DECORATIVE BOXES

SUSANNE KLØJGÅRD

CRESCENT BOOKS
NEW YORK • AVENEL, NEW JERSEY

This 1995 edition published by Crescent Books, distributed by
Random House Value Publishing, Inc.
40 Engelhard Avenue, Avenel, New Jersey 07001.

Random House
New York • Toronto • London • Sydney • Auckland

A CIP catalog record for this book is available from the Library
of Congress.

ISBN 0-517-14226-0

Printed and bound in Singapore

10 9 8 7 6 5 4 3 2 1

CONTENTS

INTRODUCTION

Boxes never fail to fascinate. There is something intriguing about them because the contents are always secret, even if only for a short time, and a pretty box can enhance the value of what is inside. We keep our most precious belongings in boxes, as well as using boxes for objects that we want to take special care of.

It is not surprising, therefore, that when we want to make a gift more personal, we place it inside a box, and what could be more personal than to use a box we have made ourselves.

Box-making is an ancient craft that used to be practised across the world. In the days before cupboards and chests of drawers were common, boxes were used to hold a variety of objects – anything from hats, to blankets, to jewellery.

In recent years there has been a revival of interest in box-making. This is not only because of the uniquely personal touch that a hand-made box will give to a gift, no matter how small, but also because there is something truly rewarding about making a box.

The boxes described in this book range from a simple pencil box to a more complicated needlework box with inserted trays. There is also a games chest and a magic box. Box-making is not just for adults, though. It's an exciting pastime for older children, too, which is why you will find several ideas for small,

relatively straightforward boxes, instructions for an Advent calendar and much, much more.

The first section describes the materials and tools you will need. We then look at the principles underlying all box-making, so it is a good idea to read the book right through, even if you do not want to make some of the boxes in the early chapters, so that you understand the basics of what is involved. In addition, the degree of difficulty increases throughout the book, with the first projects being easier to make than the ones in the last chapter. Where necessary, however, you will find that there are cross-references to procedures and methods that were explained in earlier projects. Next to each project title is a number in brackets, which indicates the page on which you will find a colour illustration of the box to guide you.

You can also, of course, combine elements from the projects to make up your own designs. You do not have to keep to the templates and the patterns illustrated here. Once you have mastered the basic techniques, you will be able to choose your own style and adapt the methods accordingly.

You will find lots of tips and advice on the following pages to help you make really professional-looking boxes, and I hope that the ideas in this book will inspire both adults and children.

Have fun!

Susanne Kløjgård

Susanne Kløjgård

MATERIALS

This chapter includes information on the materials used to make the boxes described in this book. You will find it helpful if you read this section so that you become familiar with the terms and materials that we will use before you begin. You will find all sorts of different weights, finishes and colours of card and paper in stationery shops and shops that sell artists' materials.

CARDBOARD

You will find that there are several grades of cardboard that can be used. For example, white glazed card has a fine, smooth surface, and it does not crack or wear around the edges. Cardboard can be measured in millimetres, but it is more often sold according to weight – grams per square metre (usually written as gsm or g/m²). The main kinds of card that can be used for box-making include:

Bookbinder's board This grey board is, unusually, not sold by weight. It is about 2mm (1/10in) thick and consists of a single, thick layer, which makes it hang together better than card made from several layers glued and compressed together. It is very stiff and is, therefore, ideal for folders and other flat articles.

Box card This card, which is 1mm (1/20in) thick and 400–500gsm, is ideal for smaller boxes – those less than 15cm (6in) in diameter – or for the bases of other boxes. Although it is called "card", it is actually thick enough to qualify as cardboard, and usually only one side is smooth.

Calendar board This kind of card, which is 2mm (1/10in) thick and 1000gsm, is useful for boxes that are 30–40cm (12–16in) across.

Display card This card, which is 1.5mm (1/16in) thick and 780gsm, is used for larger boxes.

TIP

Smaller boxes made from lighter weight card can be cut out with sharp scissors. However, the best way to obtain an accurate edge is to cut cardboard with a craft knife or scalpel, held against a metal rule or metal-edged ruler. When you cut, hold the knife as shown in the illustration – that is, hold it at a slight angle and use a large area of the blade so that it does not wear down so quickly. If the card is very thick, you may not be able to cut it in one go. Make sure that the ruler is in exactly the same position for each cut.

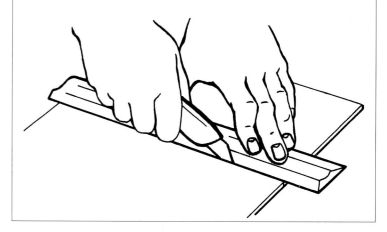

PAPER

You will need paper to cover and decorate the boxes. There is a wide range of colours and patterns available, and when you are selecting a paper it is a good idea to look for one that will be appropriate to the kind of box you are making and that will create the right impression. Do you want the box to look amusing or sophisticated or modern?

Brown wrapping paper It is a good idea to apply a base cover of brown paper all over a box before you begin to stick on more decorative gift-wrapping paper. You can also give a box extra strength by applying adhesive to strips of brown paper and using these instead of lengths of adhesive tape, which does tend to lose its sticking power over time. Pieces of brown wrapping paper can also be used to conceal the edges of adhesive tape, if you are using a lightweight covering paper.

Copying paper Stationers stock a range of colours, although most of them are pastel shades.

Foil Gold and silver foil is available in sheets. Make sure you buy paper-backed foils, or you will not be able to glue it to the card.

Gift-wrapping paper Stationers and department stores stock wide ranges, which are often available in rolls or as single sheets. Wherever possible, buy sheets of paper because the paper in rolls is thinner and less robust, and there is always a danger that it will curl when it is glued. Some museums and shops that specialize in reproduction artefacts also sell gift-wrapping paper with classical designs, and these are always worth looking out for.

Glazed paper Paper with a high-glaze, glossy finish will give a smooth, restrained look to a box.

Hand-made paper Use hand-made paper to give your boxes an extra stylish, uniquely personal finish. One problem is that hand-made papers tend to dissolve when glue is applied directly to the surface, but you can cover the box with a coat of glue under a very lightweight paper, and the hand-made paper can be pressed down on the lighter paper to which it will adhere.

Marbled paper You can colour your own paper by dripping paints, inks and dyes into water baths and trailing the colours through the water before placing your paper on the surface. There are several books on patterning paper in this way, and sheets coloured in this way are ideal for decorating boxes.

GLUE, PASTE AND TAPE

It is worth remembering that glue and paste are not the same thing. Glue is stronger and is used to stick card and paper together at the corners. Paste is used when you cover a box with paper. The distinction between paste and glue is observed in all the instructions in this book – if the directions say use paste, you must use paste; if they say use glue, you must use glue!

Adhesive tape You will need adhesive tape to hold the corners of small boxes together. Make sure that it is as fine as possible so that it does not cause unsightly ridges when you apply a covering of paper.

Glue stick You can use a glue stick instead of paste when you are covering a box or card with paper. It dries more quickly than paste, but you must use it sparingly and you must make sure that you spread it out to the very edge of the paper.

Linen tape This tape, which is available in two widths, 18mm and 38mm (about ¾in and 1½in), can be used to make hinges. You can also use passe-partout.

Mull This thin, soft, plain muslin is traditionally used in bookbinding to hold the spine of a book in place. You can use it instead of tape to create hinged lids; see, for example, the needlework box on page 66.

PVA adhesive This is non-toxic and easy to work with. Although it dries quickly (within 10 minutes), it is water-soluble and fairly easy to remove. Use a spreader or your finger to apply a smooth line of adhesive right along the edges you want to glue together.

Wallpaper paste When you are covering a box with paper, use wallpaper paste. It is cheap to buy and easy to use, and any excess paste that appears around the edges can be wiped away and will not leave a mark. Use a flat brush, about 18mm (¾in) wide, to apply the paste and always cover your work surface with old newspaper. Wash the brush thoroughly in clean water when you have finished.

TIP

When you mix wallpaper paste, use about 1 teaspoon of paste granules to 0.5 litres (1 pint) of cold water. Sprinkle the paste over the water while you stir. Leave to stand for about 15 minutes and then stir again before use to avoid lumps forming. You can keep any excess in a screw-top jar.

TOOLS AND EQUIPMENT

It is important that you have the right tools to begin with, and the most important ones are listed here. You will find most of these items around your home, so you probably will not need to spend too much money to begin with.

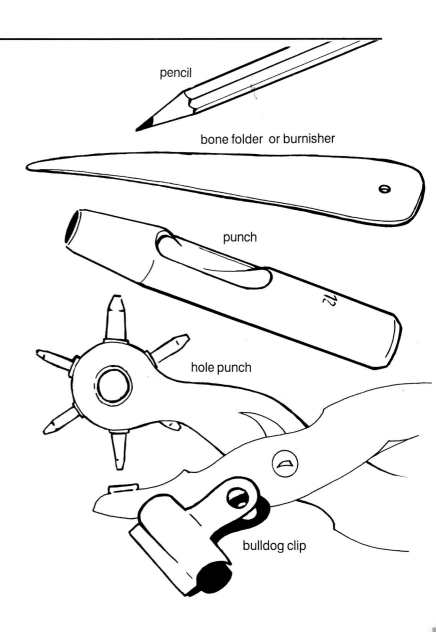

pencil

bone folder or burnisher

punch

hole punch

bulldog clip

Bone folder or burnisher This useful little tool has a point at one end, which is used for scoring fold lines in paper or lightweight card to make it easier to fold and bend. It is not suitable for thick card, when you should use the end of a scissor blade or the point of a knife – but take care that you do not go right through. You will find your folding stick useful when you are covering a box with paper – it will help you smooth over the paper to remove creases and air bubbles. If you do not have a burnisher, use a teaspoon.

Bulldog clips You will find a range of sizes in most stationers. Use them to hold paper and card together until the adhesive dries.

Compasses These are essential if you are making circular boxes. If you intend to make a lot of boxes, you might want to buy some special compasses that hold a blade so that you can cut smooth curves.

Craft knife The best kind, and the most economical, are the ones with the blade held in the body of the knife. You break off sections of the blade as they become blunt. You can use a scalpel instead. Remember that both craft knives and scalpel blades are sharp and can be dangerous. Always use them carefully.

Cutting mat Shops that sell artists' materials stock special cutting mats, which are made of a rubberized material so that they do not slip and which are specially treated so that the cuts "close up". Some of these mats have vertical and horizontal lines on them, which help you line up your ruler and set square.

Hole punch The plier type of hole punch is the most useful for making small holes.

Paint If you use paint for decorating your boxes, make sure you choose a kind that covers well and that has a good, strong surface that will not rub off when your box is opened and shut. Water-based acrylic paints are widely available and are easy to work with.

Pencil This is essential for drawing. It should be quite hard and always well sharpened so that you can draw fine, neat lines.

Punch Tube punches are small chiselling tools with circular heads that are used for making holes. They are available with diameters of 2–45mm ($1/16$ – $1\frac{3}{4}$in).

Ruler You will need a ruler both for measuring and for cutting against. The best kinds are metal, and in any case, if you use a ruler for cutting against you will need one with a metal edge. The most suitable ones are rubber-backed so that they do not slip as you press against them.

Scissors Sharp scissors are essential. Ideally you should have a large pair for cutting cardboard and a small pair for paper and lightweight card. You will also find the tip of a scissor blade invaluable for scoring fold lines. Do not use these scissors for cutting other things.

Set square You will find a set square invaluable for making sure that the corners of your boxes are absolutely accurate.

Tape measure Sometimes a tape measure is more useful than a ruler, especially when you need to measure around curved objects.

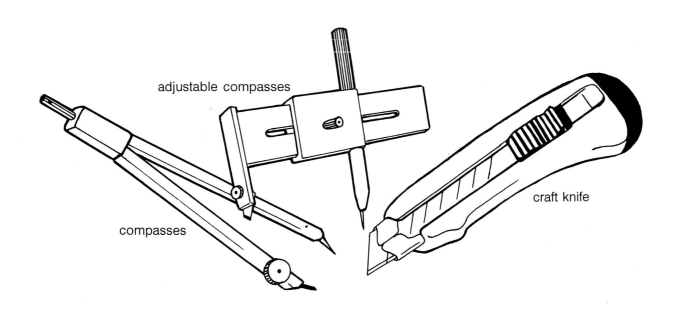

adjustable compasses

compasses

craft knife

HOW TO MAKE A BOX

You can make boxes in almost any shape you wish. The simplest kind, of course, are four-sided boxes, which can be as large or as small, as low or as high as you want and either square or rectangular. The two main methods for making four-sided boxes – by folding and by cutting – are described below. You can also easily make circular boxes, and the basic method is described on pages 18–19. Once you have mastered the technique, you can make hexagonal, star- and moon-shaped boxes (see pages 31– 6).

THE FOLDING METHOD

This method is best if you are making a fairly small box. Use box card and decide on the dimensions. We have made a box that has a base measuring 50 x 50mm (2 x 2in) with sides that are 60mm (2½in) high.

1 Draw the base on a square of cardboard. Measure and check the angles carefully, using a set square to make sure that they are all 90 degrees. If one of them is evenly slightly wrong, the whole box will be thrown out of true.

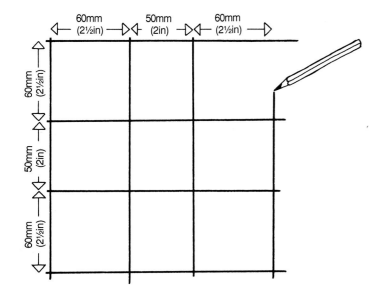

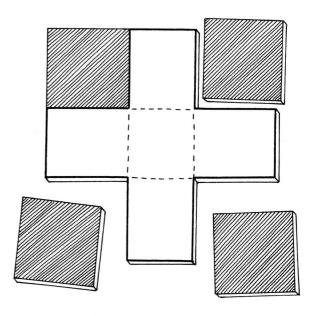

2 Measure the height of the box for all four sides and draw in the lines as shown. You will have nine squares in all, which look rather like a section of a chessboard.

3 Use a sharp pair of scissors or a craft knife to cut out the overall shape and then to cut away the corners. Cutting in towards the centre from the edge will give the neatest, sharpest angles. Your piece of cardboard will now look like a cross.

4 Use the point of the bone folder or burnisher or the tip of a scissor blade to score the four lines around the base.

5 Bend the sides upwards so that the score lines are on the outside. If you have been careful, the sides of the box should be level.

6 Use small pieces of adhesive tape to hold the sides together. Place the tape as near to the top of the sides as possible to make the box stable, and smooth the tape down neatly so that it will not be visible through the covering material.

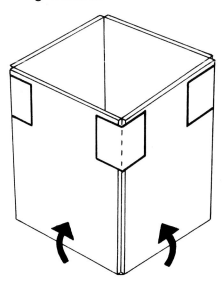

TIP
If you want to strengthen the box, paste a strip of brown wrapping paper around it. Make the strip the same height as the box and it should be very slightly longer than the distance around the four sides. The brown paper has the advantage that it will help conceal the edges of the adhesive tape, which can be visible when you cover a box with lightweight paper.

You can make a lid for the box in the same way as you made the base. However, it should be slightly larger so that it slips easily over the sides of the base section. If you have used box card, which is 1mm ($^1/_{20}$in) thick, and intend covering the box with ordinary gift-wrapping paper, you should add an extra 3mm ($^1/_8$in) to all the dimensions. The base of the box would, therefore, be 53 x 53mm ($2^1/_8$ x $2^1/_8$in).

When you are estimating the size of the lid, a useful guide is to say that it should be three cardboard thicknesses larger, which allows room for two sides of cardboard and space to allow the lid to slide on and off easily. If you use a thicker covering paper, you should allow four cardboard thicknesses extra.

The lid has sides that are the same depth as the base, and this will give a box that closes to form a tight unit. You could also make a lid that comes to about halfway down the sides of the base section by making it about 3cm (1¼in) deep.

Make the lid in the same way as the base. Instructions on covering box and lid are on page 22.

THE CUTTING METHOD

This is the method to use for larger boxes made from thicker card, such as display card, which is at least 1.5mm (¹⁄₁₆in) thick. As with the folding method, you must first decide how large you want to the box to be. We have made one that has a base measuring 100 x 100mm (4 x 4in) and sides 60mm (2½in) high.

Assemble the lid in the same way, but make sure that the dimensions are slightly larger. The top should be three thicknesses of cardboard bigger than the base, and if you use a fairly sturdy covering material or if the lid is to cover the sides of the box completely, you should make it four thicknesses of cardboard bigger.

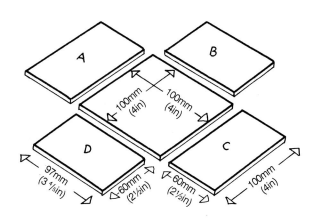

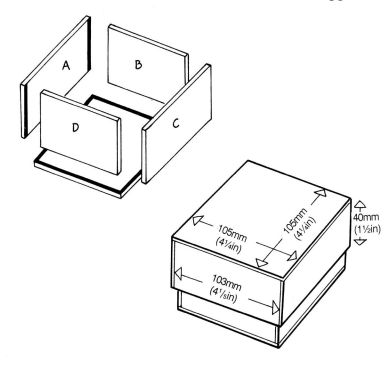

1 Cut out all the pieces, using a craft knife and a metal-edged ruler.

2 Glue the sides to the base. This will mean that the internal dimensions are less than the external ones – that is, allowing a 3mm (about ¹⁄₈in) reduction all round, the base will measure 97 x 97mm (3 ⁷⁄₈ x 3 ⁷⁄₈in).

3 Use your finger or a spatular to apply a thin line of glue to the edges shown in black in the illustration.

4 Position the sides so that they are at right-angles to the base. Begin with long side (A), then position the two short sides (B and D), and finally put the second long side (C) in place. You may have to support them until the glue is dry.

TIP

Before you cover the box and the lid with decorative paper, it is a good idea to try the lid on the base. It should not be so loose that it falls off, but it should not be so tight that it gets stuck.

How to make a box (see pages 14-19).

MAKING A BOX WITH A LINER

The lid does not always have to go over the bottom section of the box in order to fit snugly. If you glue on a small liner or bezel inside the base, the lid will sit on the lip of the liner, which will be higher than the sides of the base.

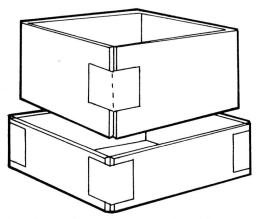

You can use either the folding method (page 14) or the cutting method (page 16), but the base and the lid should be exactly the same size.

Make the bezel from a strip of lightweight card – box card, for example – that is slightly deeper than the height of the base of your box.

1 If your box is square, measure one of the internal sides of the base of the box and subtract 1mm ($\frac{1}{20}$in).

2 Use a pencil to mark this length on the strip of card, and then measure off three more equal lengths. Cut off any remaining card.

3 Use the point of a bone folder or a scissor blade to score the lines you have marked.

4 Fold the strip, check the fit inside the box and tape the loose corner together.

If your box is rectangular, you should measure out the dimensions of a long and a short side, deducting 1mm ($\frac{1}{20}$in) from each dimension.

The lid should fit neatly over the rim formed by the liner, moving up and down easily but not being so loose that it falls off. If you find it difficult to make the liner fit, cut out four separate pieces and glue them individually in place. Do not glue the liner in position until you have covered the box (see page 26).

MAKING A CIRCULAR BOX

Don't be put off from making circular boxes. If you follow the instructions here you will find that the whole process is much easier than you might think.

When you begin to cut and bend cardboard, you will discover that it will be much more difficult to work with in one direction than in the other. Do not force the card, but always try to curve it in the direction that offers least resistance. If you do not, the cardboard will develop small cracks that will be impossible to rectify or disguise.

TIP

You do not always have to make circular boxes from scratch. All kinds of things are packaged with cardboard tubes – from kitchen towels to toilet paper – and you can often buy cardboard tubes from shops specializing in art and craft supplies.

You can also buy large, round boxes for storing hats, and these are ready for covering with paper and decorating in your own style.

1 Use a pair of compasses to draw two circles with the same diameter on to thick card. Cut them out. If the edges are a little ragged and frayed, smooth them with fine sandpaper.

2 Decide how high you want the box to be and cut a strip of box card to that width, remembering to cut it so that the card will curve easily.

3 Cut the card so that it is 18mm (about ¾in) longer than the circumference of the circles. Use a tape measure to measure the distance accurately.

4 Stick small lengths of narrow, low-tack adhesive tape all around the edge of the base circle so that about half each piece extends beyond the edge of the base. Use narrow tape so that it adheres neatly to the curved edge and does not crease. Turn over the base so that the sticky side of the tape is facing upwards.

5 Apply a narrow line of adhesive along one long edge the side piece, and then begin to fit the side piece, holding it in place as you work with the adhesive tape.

6 When you have attached the side piece almost all the way round, apply some adhesive to the free short end, then finish positioning the card. Hold the ends together with a clothes peg or bulldog clip and use some more pieces of adhesive tape to hold the side in place near to the base.

7 Make a lid in the same way, adjusting the depth of the side as you wish. Make sure that the diameters of the two circles are the same. It is very easy for the strip to contract a little as you work.

8 When the glue is dry, remove the bulldog clips or clothes pegs and the strips of adhesive tape.

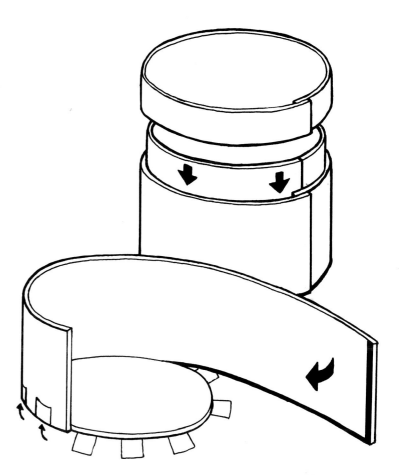

MAKING A LINER

To hold the lid firmly in place, make a liner as described on page 18. The liner should be slightly deeper than the bottom half of the box, and you can use a tape measure to find the exact length of the internal circumference of the base. Initially, make the liner slightly longer than you need and place it inside the box so that you can trim it to fit. The lid should fit snugly over the lip but should not be so loose that it falls off or so tight that it cannot be replaced easily. Do not glue the liner in place until you have covered the box (see page 27).

19

HOW TO COVER A BOX

This chapter includes everything you need to know about covering the boxes you have made, and it is worth reading the pages that follow before you begin work, just to familiarize yourself with the procedure.

You should cover your boxes not only to make them look attractive but also to strengthen them. Make sure that the paper you use covers all the joins, both to conceal them and make them stable.

As we have seen (page 11), wallpaper paste is the cheapest and easiest to use. The paste makes the paper pliable and easy to work with, and it dries so that you can adjust the position slightly. When you apply the paste, use a flat brush and work from the centre to the edges. Take care not to apply too much and try not to get paste on the front. Wipe up any spots straightaway. Keep a damp cloth near at hand so that you can keep your fingers clean and mop up any spots of paste, which will spoil the appearance of your box.

Use the bowl of a teaspoon or a burnisher to smooth the paper carefully whenever you apply a new piece. You must avoid creases and air bubbles, and if your wallpaper paste is a bit lumpy, remove the lumps from the surface of the paper or they will be visible when the paste is dry.

As soon as the water in the paste comes into contact with the cardboard it will make it pliable and liable to stretching and contracting. You must, therefore, always cover both sides to stop it from bending and becoming distorted. It is also a good idea to let the box dry under light pressure.

Covering boxes (see pages 20-7).

COVERING THE EDGES

It is not absolutely essential to cover the sides of a box with paper, although they often look more attractive. One of the easiest ways of finishing off a box is to cover the sides with paper or paint and then to paste strips of paper or tape along all the edges. The Chinese Boxes illustrated on page 49 show how the edging can add the perfect finishing touch.

If you want to cover a box completely with paper before applying edging strips, it is a good idea to make templates of the external and internal sides, base and lid. Cut out the paper from the templates, cover it carefully with a smooth layer of paste and lay each piece over the cardboard so that the edges align perfectly. Use your burnisher or the bowl of a teaspoon to smooth out any creases and wipe away any excess paste. Leave the box to dry.

Alternatively, just paint the outside and inside of the box. Leave to dry.

1 To edge a medium-sized box, measure all the sides that need to be covered and cut lengths of edging paper that are 12mm (½in) wide. If the cardboard or the covering paper are thick, the strips used for the rim should be a little bit wider than those used for the inside and the corners.

2 Fold a strip in half, apply paste and, beginning at one end, press the strip into position.

3 The finished box will look smarter if you cut off the end of each strip at an angle so that the corners where the strips meet form neat mitres.

4 The ends of the interior strips should also be cut at an angle so that the paper does not overlap and cause unsightly bumps in the corners.

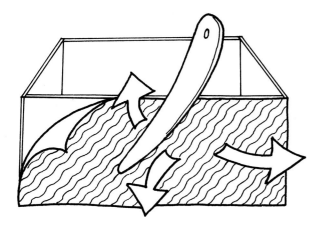

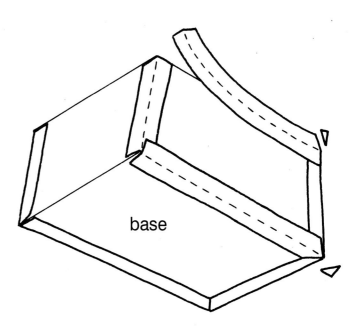

base

If you do not want to have to use edging strips on the outside of a folded box, you could try cutting out the covering paper so that it is slightly larger than the side to be covered and will wrap around the corners, edges and rims.

Covering the Inside
Always cover the inside of a folded box before you assemble it.

1 When you have cut out the sections for the base and lid, use these as templates for the covering paper but make them about 2mm ($^1/_{10}$in) less all round because the paper will stretch slightly when it is moistened by the paste, and it is important that the paper does not protrude beyond the edges of the card.

2 Apply paste to the back of the paper and position it over the card.

3 Use your burnisher to smooth the paper and wipe away any excess paste.

4 Leave the card to dry, then score in the fold lines on the side that you have not covered.

5 Fold up the sides and hold with adhesive tape.

Covering the Outside
You can use the unassembled base and lid sections as templates for the paper that will cover the outside, but you must allow an extra 12mm ($^1/_2$in) on all top edges and along both edges of two opposite sides .

1 Draw the position of the base lightly in pencil before you apply paste.

2 Apply a coat of paste, position the box then fold up the two sides with extra flaps. These are labelled A and C on the illustration. Fold the flaps around the corners and over the rim.

3 Smooth all surfaces with a burnisher and wipe away any excess paste.

4 Fold up the two remaining sides. You may need to apply a little more paste if it has dried.

5 Cover the lid in the same way, put the lid on the box and leave to dry under slight pressure.

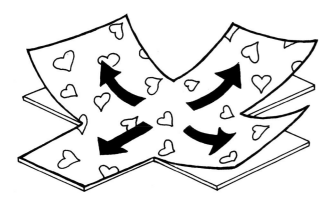

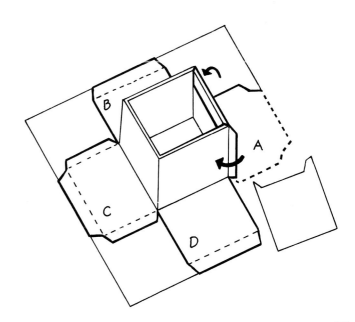

Make the box as described on page 16. Boxes made in this way are often too large to cover with a single sheet, and it is usually better to cut long strips that will run right around the outside and inside of the box and use separate squares or rectangles of the same paper for the lid and base.

Covering the Inside

1 Cut a rectangle that is 2mm (¹/₁₀in) wider and longer than the base and trim the corners to a neat angle.

2 Apply a coat of paste to the paper and place it carefully in the bottom of the box. Use your burnisher to smooth it so that there are no creases or air bubbles. Wipe away any excess glue that oozes out. The paper should be positioned so that the turned-up edge is the same height all round.

3 Cut a strip about 2mm (¹/₁₀in) less than the internal height of the box to allow for the stretching that will happen when you apply the paste and 12mm (½in) longer than the length of all four sides.

4 Apply a coat of paste to the strip and place it inside the box so that it runs all the way round. Make sure that it goes right down to the base and covers the turned-up edge from the paper on the bottom of the box. Use your burnisher to eliminate bubbles and creases, and wipe away any excess paste.

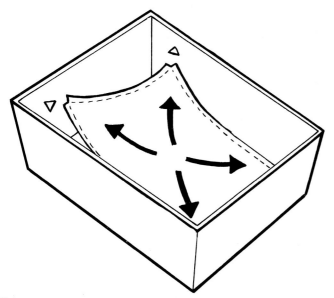

TIP

Your box will look more professional if the paper ends precisely in one corner. Place one end of the strip neatly in the corner but do not press it down. When you are happy that the sides are neatly and smoothly covered and that the paper is correctly placed, lift up the first end (A in the illustration below) and fold the other end (B) into and around the corner. Smooth down end A firmly.

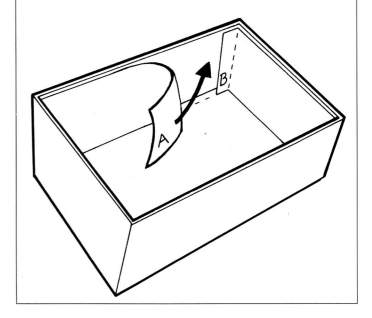

Covering the Outside

There are two ways to cover the outside of a box. You can either use a single piece as you did on the inside or you can use separate pieces. If you use a single strip, measure right around all four sides of the base or lid and add on 12mm (½in). The paper should be 18mm (about ¾in) wider than the depth of the sides.

1 Draw a pencil line 12mm (½in) from one long edge so that you can position the box centrally on the strip.

2 Apply a coat of paste to the paper and place it on the box so that the end of the strip is at a corner.

3 Cut small triangles at the top and bottom of each corner.

4 Fold the edge of the strip over the base of the box, using your burnisher to make sure that the paper is smooth and crease-free.

5 Bend the top edge over the rim of the box. Make sure the surface is smooth and wipe away any excess paste.

6 Cut out squares or rectangles of paper to cover the base and top of the box and paste them down.

If your box is so large that you cannot find any suitable paper that will cover the sides in a single strip, you will have to cover each side individually. Although this may seem time-consuming, it does offer greater possibilities in terms of decoration, as we shall see.

1 Cover the long sides first. Measure them carefully and draw the outlines on the cover paper, adding 12mm (½in) all round. Cut out the pieces.

2 Measure the two shorter sides and draw the outlines on the cover paper, but here you need add on the extra 12mm (½in) to the top and bottom.

3 Apply paste to the paper for one of the long edges and position it on the box. Cut the corners as shown and bend in the small flaps, then the longer ones, so that the paper lies smoothly around the corners. Repeat with the other long side.

4 Paste one of the short pieces and position it carefully. Cut small triangles from the bottom corners only.

5 Cut out and paste on pieces to cover the base and the lid.

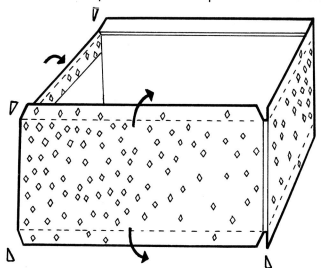

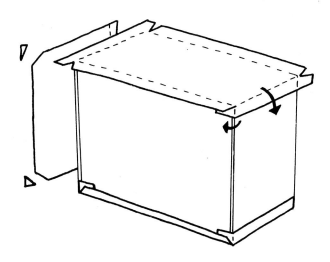

COVERING BOXES WITH LINERS

If you have made a box with a liner to form a lip or bezel to hold the lid (see page 18), you can cover it in almost the same way as you would a normal cut or folded box. Inside, however, you need only cover the bottom of the box, because the sides will be covered by the liner, which will be covered before it is glued in place.

Covering the Inside

1 Cut a strip 12mm (½in) longer than the internal length and 2mm (1/10in) narrower than the depth.

2 Apply some paste and position the strip inside the liner.

3 Smooth it down carefully with a burnisher, taking especial care in the corners.

Covering the Outside

1 Take a strip of paper that is 12mm (½in) longer than the length around the liner. The paper should be as wide as the depth of the liner that protrudes above the edge of the box **plus** 18mm (about ¾in).

2 Draw a pencil line 12mm (½in) from one long edge. Apply a coat of paste and position the liner so that the top edge aligns with the pencil line. Make sure that the cover paper ends neatly at a corner.

3 Cut small triangles from each corner and fold the flaps inwards.

4 When the paste is dry, apply some adhesive to the lower outside edge of the liner and place it inside the box. Hold it in place with clips until the glue is dry.

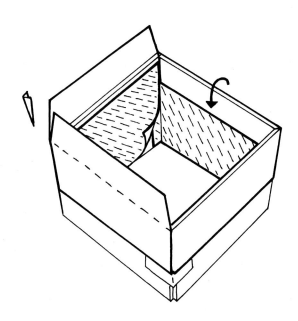

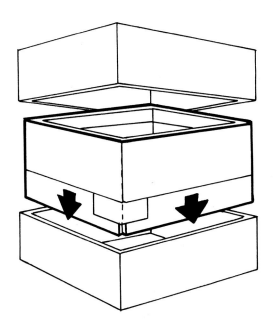

COVERING CIRCULAR BOXES

Make a box as described on pages 18–19, but unlike square boxes you should cover the outside first.

Covering the Outside

1 Cut a strip that is 18mm (about ¾in) wider than the depth of the side of your box and 12mm (½in) longer.

2 Draw a pencil line 12mm (½in) from one long edge and apply a coat of paste.

3 Using the pencil line as a guide, paste the strip right around the side of the box, using your burnisher to smooth out any creases and air bubbles.

4 At the open end, bend the paper over so that it lies neatly inside the box.

5 At the other end, make a series of cuts or notches, no more than 12mm (½in) apart, all the way around and up to the edge of the side.

6 Press down each flap of paper in turn, applying more paste if necessary, with your burnisher.

7 Cut out a circle to the same diameter as the base and paste it down to cover the little flaps. Wipe away any excess paste and leave to dry. Repeat for the lid.

Covering the Inside

1 Cut out a circle with the same diameter as the inside of the base **plus** 2mm (¹/₁₀in). Paste the circle and press it into position, making sure that the turned-up edge is even all round and pressed firmly into place with your burnisher.

2 Cut a strip that is 12mm (½in) longer than the internal circumference of the box and that is 5mm (about ¼in) narrower than its depth.

3 Paste the strip and position it so that it covers the upturned edge of the piece covering the base. Use your burnisher to smooth out all creases. Wipe away any excess paste.

If you want to keep the lid of your box in place, bore two holes at opposite sides of the base, just below the edge of lid, and run a cord through. See page 41.

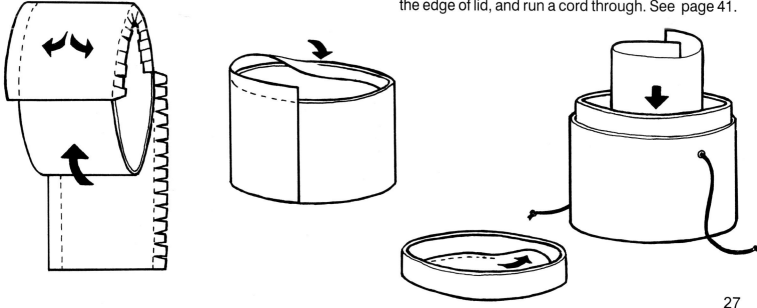

LIQUORICE ALLSORTS BOXES

These boxes have been decorated so that they look like Liquorice Allsorts, which makes them perfect for gifts for anyone who has a sweet tooth – especially if they are filled with real Liquorice Allsorts.

SQUARE BOXES [29]

Make the boxes following the directions for the folded box with liner on pages 14 and 18, and line the inside of the boxes as described on page 26.

Covering the Outside
Use pink, yellow and white paper to cover the box and strips of black paper for the liquorice.

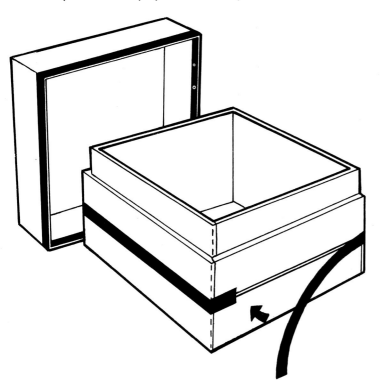

1 Cover the top of the lid and the bottom of the base with coloured paper. You should measure the paper so that the amount turned up around the base and up the sides of the box is equal to the depth of the sides of the lid. Trim the corners so that the angles are smooth and neat.

2 Cut a strip of coloured paper, 12mm (½in) longer than the distance around the outside of the base and about half the depth of the base, and paste it to the top of the base.

3 Cut two strips of black paper, one about twice as wide as the other. Paste the narrower strip right around the base so that it covers the join between the two coloured papers. Make sure the strip starts and ends at a corner.

4 Use the wider strip to cover the rim of the lid – remember to fold it in two lengthways before you apply the paste so that it is easier to position. Use your burnisher to press the strip firmly down on the inside, especially into the corners.

Square and circular Liquorice Allsorts boxes (pages 28-30).

There are lots of ways you can decorate circular boxes to make them resemble Liquorice Allsorts. The boxes illustrated here were made as described on pages 18–19. Here are a few ideas for covering them, but you can choose the colours that match your own favourites from a box of sweets.

The tall black box is simply covered with glossy paper, which is ideal for liquorice, with a circle of white paper stuck in the centre of the lid. You could repeat this on the base if you wish or simply cover the base with a circle of black.

The orange box has a circle of black paper stuck in the centre of the lid and of the base. Try to get the proportions right when you measure the circles.

Finally, the lid of the green box was covered with shiny black paper, and this was covered with circles in different shades of blue and green, drawn around a coin as a template.

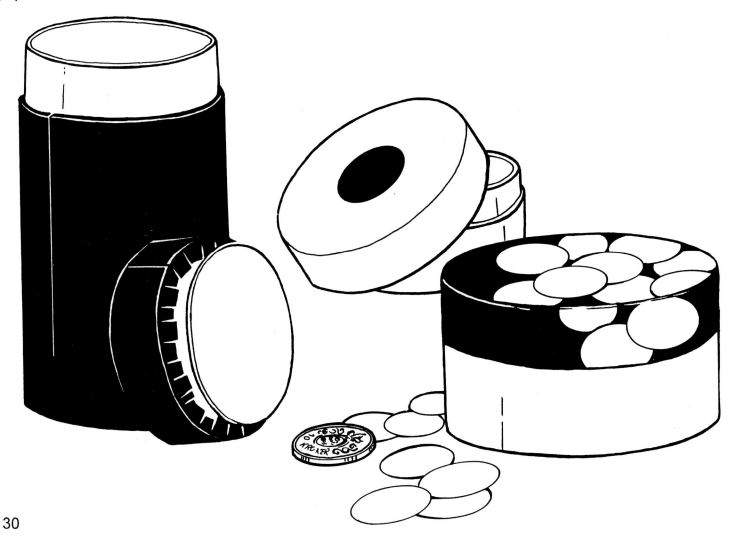

SUN, MOON AND STAR BOXES

You can make boxes in almost any shape you want – they don't have to be circular or square. Experiment with different combinations of techniques and you will be surprised at the variety of boxes you will make.

One problem that can arise with unusually shaped boxes is to get the lid to fit accurately. This is largely because the cardboard tends to become pliable and stretchy when it is moistened. Practice will make perfect, though, so do not give up if your first attempts don't work as well you had hoped.

SUN BOX [33]

This box is based on the standard circular box described on pages 18–19.

Covering the Lid
The basic procedure is as described on page 27. The measurements here are for a box with a diameter of 26cm (10¼in); adjust these for smaller or larger boxes. We used a gold paper to look like the sun's rays.

1 Cut out a circle of white paper the same diameter as the top of the lid and paste it in position.

2 Cut a strip of gold paper 12mm (½in) longer than the circumference of the lid and about 6cm (2½in) deeper than the lid.

3 On the back of the paper draw two pencil lines, one 12mm (½in) from the bottom edge and the other about 5cm (2in) from the top edge. Along the top edge draw a series of triangles with a base of about 12mm (½in) as shown. Cut these out.

4 Apply a coat of paste to the paper and position it around the lid, with the tops of the triangles pointing upwards and with the edge of the lid against the other pencil line.

5 Turn the 12mm (½in) edge down around the rim of the box and press it smoothly and firmly into position.

6 Press down the teeth around the top of the lid one by one. You may have to add a little more paste if it has started to dry. Press them down smoothly and firmly over the lid. Wipe away any excess paste.

Cover the inside of the lid and the inside and outside of the base as described on page 27.

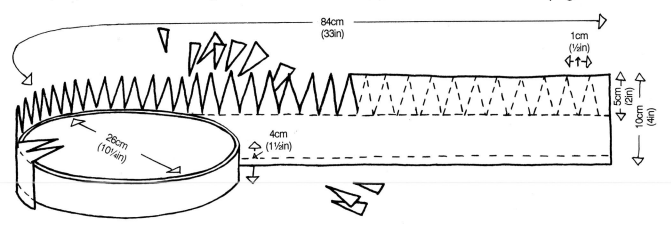

The principle behind the moon-shaped boxes is very similar to that used to make circular boxes (see pages 18–19), and you should use the same type of cardboard and work with it in the same way.

1 Using the templates on page 35, cut out two identical crescent-shapes in thick cardboard. If the edges are frayed, smooth them with fine sandpaper.

2 The sides are made in two separate sections. The templates show the length of the two sides for each size shown, but if you have used a different sized base, use a tape measure to measure the length of the curves. Cut out a rectangle for each side; the vertical dimensions should be the height of the base and depth of the lid combined. Cut the rectangle in half lengthways to the required depths.

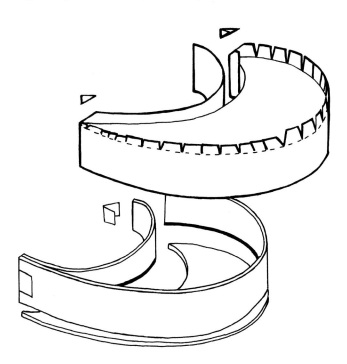

3 Use adhesive and small strips of adhesive tape as described on page 19 to glue the two sides to the base; repeat for the lid. Don't forget to glue the ends of the front and back sections together.

Covering the Outside

1 Cut a piece of paper 18mm (about ¾in) wider and 18mm (about ¾in) longer than the longer of the two sides.

2 If you wish, draw a pencil line 12mm (½in) in from one long edge. Apply paste to the paper and position the box so that it is fairly central on the paper, lining it up with your pencil line if you wish. Fold the paper around the front corners and smooth it down.

3 Cut the corners of the paper at the edge that will be folded over inside the box. Smooth it firmly over the edge, adding more paste if necessary.

4 At the side that will be turned over the base or lid, make a series of small, evenly spaced cuts around the edge. Fold each one down in turn, adding more paste if necessary, and smooth them down with your burnisher. Trim off the excess paper in the corners.

5 For the shorter side, cut a piece of paper that is the same length as, but 18mm (about ¾in) deeper than, the side.

6 Apply paste and position the paper centrally on the curve. Fold over the inside edge.

7 Make a series of evenly spaced cuts on the other side and press them down over the back of the base or the lid. Add more paste if necessary.

8 Finally, use the template to cut out two crescents to cover the top of the lid and the base of the lid.

Sun, moon and star boxes (pages 31-6).

Covering the Inside

1 Use the template to cut out two crescents for the inside of the lid and the bottom of the base.

2 Cut a strip for the inside of the lid. This should be a little narrower than the depth of the lid and 12mm (½in) longer than the overall length. Apply paste and press it into position, taking especial care to press it smoothly into the corners and along the bottom edge.

3 Make a liner as described on page 18, making it in two parts, and cover it as described on page 26.

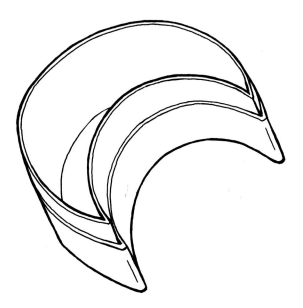

STAR BOX [33]

The star box has so many sides that it can give a little. It does not need a liner to hold the lid in place – just push in the sides as you press the lid down over the base.

1 Use the template on page 35 to cut out two stars from display card. If you want to make a larger box, enlarge the template on a photocopier or by the grid method.

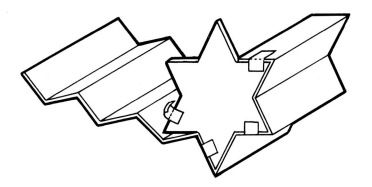

2 Calculate the length of the edge strip by measuring one of the sides of the star and multiplying by 12. In our example, the side of the star is 30mm (1¼in), giving an edge piece of 360mm (15in). If you want to make a tall box, similar to the one illustrated on page 33, the edge piece should be 180mm (7¼in) wide.

3 Measure accurately the divisions of the side piece, drawing pencil lines to indicate where the folds should be. Use the point of a bone folder or the end of a scissor blade to score along each line on both sides of the card.

4 Cut the side piece lengthways to form the sides of the base and the edge of the lid. We made the pieces 140mm (5½in) and 40mm (1¾in) respectively.

5 Apply a thin line of glue to the edge of one of the stars and, using small pieces of adhesive tape as for a circular box (see page 19) , attach the side piece.

6 Make the lid in the same way.

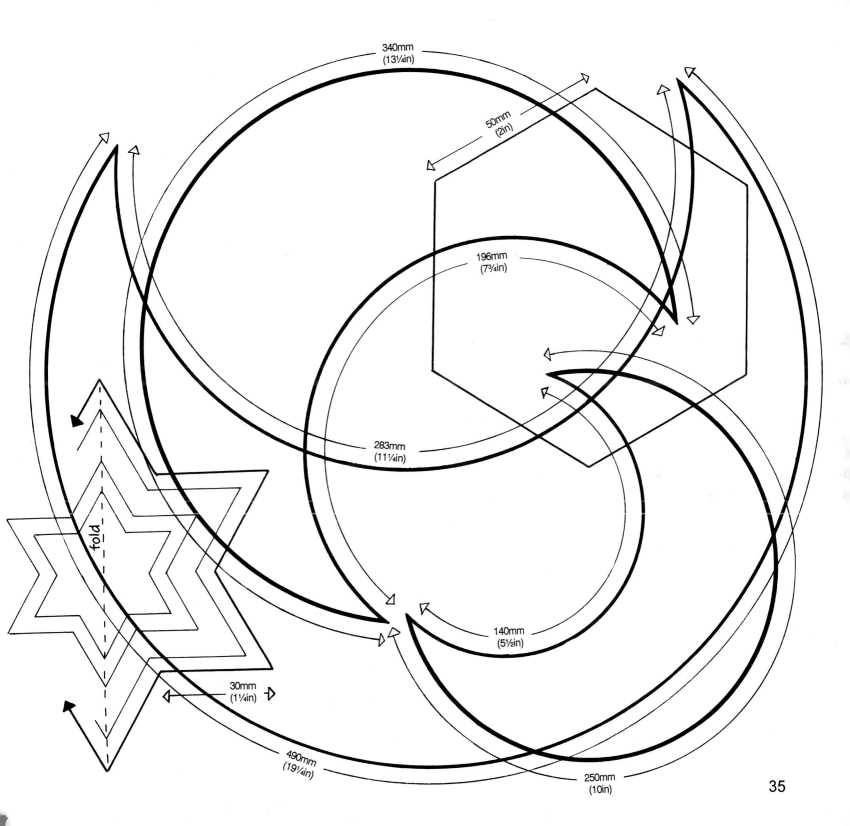

340mm
(13¼in)

50mm
(2in)

196mm
(7¾in)

283mm
(11¼in)

fold

140mm
(5½in)

30mm
(1¼in)

490mm
(19¼in)

250mm
(10in)

35

Covering the Outside

We used white and gold paper to cover the box shown on page 33 and decorated it with gold stars.

1 Cut a strip of gold paper that is 370mm (15½in) long and 12mm (½in) wide.

2 Fold the paper in half lengthways and apply a coat of paste. Attach this strip to the rim of the lid so that it protrudes by about 5mm (¼in) above the edge. Cut a notch in each of the 12 corners of the star and fold down the edges one by one.

3 Cut a strip of white paper 370mm (15½in) long and 12mm (about ½) wider than the depth of the lid.

4 Apply a coat of paste and place the paper around the sides of the lid, positioning it so that a narrow band of gold is visible around the rim. Use your burnisher to press the paper neatly into the angles.

5 You will need to cut the paper protruding above the top of the lid so that it lies flat when you bend it over. Make neat cuts at all 12 points and press down the paper along the side of each point.

6 Use the template to cut out a white star and paste it over the top of the lid to cover the turned-in edges. We decorated the top with two bands of gold paper.

7 Follow the above steps to cover the bottom part of the box, but instead of using a narrow band of gold to cover the rim of the lid, make the gold section about 55mm (2½in) deep and use a strip of white paper about 110mm (4¼in) deep for the lower section, allowing an extra 12mm (½in) to turn under at the top and bottom.

8 Paste a white star to the bottom of the base to cover the turned-in edges of the paper used on the side.

Covering the Inside

Cut out stars for the bottom and for the inside of the lid, then paste down strips to cover the sides. Use your burnisher to press the paper into the angles.

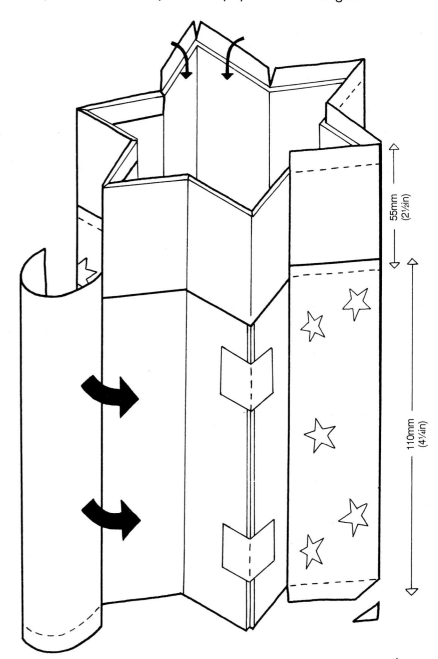

55mm (2½in)

110mm (4¼in)

Pencil holder (page 38); clipboard folder (page 40); diskette holder (page 42); pencil box (page 44).

DESK ACCESSORIES

PENCIL HOLDER [37]

This hexagonal pencil container is not difficult to make, and it is an excellent gift to make to send to someone because it can pressed flat and put into an envelope.

1 Use the template on page 35 to draw a hexagon on a piece of cardboard. Alternatively, use a pair of compasses to draw a hexagon to the size you wish.

2 You will need six side pieces. We used sides measuring 50 x 140mm (2 x 5½in). If you have drawn your own hexagon, make sure that the short sides are the same length as the sides of the hexagon and that the height is in proportion to the width.

3 Use linen tape or passe-partout to join the side pieces together. The tape will function as a hinge and should be attached to what will be the outside of the container. So that the finished container will fold up, you should leave about 2mm (¹/₁₀in) between each piece. Make sure the gap is even by placing a thick piece of card between each side piece as you apply the tape (see illustration). The tape should fold around the top and bottom edges by 12mm (½in).

4 Cover each side piece. The covering paper should turn over the top and bottom edges by 12mm (½in) but the width of each panel will depend on how much of the tape you want to be visible.

5 Use a single piece of paper to cover the inside. Cut a piece of paper that is 12mm (½in) longer than the inside measurement but 5mm (¼in) shorter, so that the turned-down edges of the paper used for the outside are visible. If you are using the template on page 35, the paper for the inside should be about 310 x 130mm (12¼ x 5¼in).

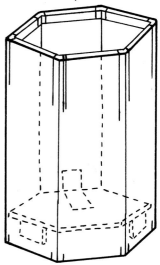

6 Make supports for the base by cutting out three pieces of thick cardboard, each 10 x 30mm (½ x 1¼in), and glue these pieces inside the bottom of the holder, attaching them to alternate panels.

8 Cover the base with paper if you wish, then push it down inside the container so that it rests on the cardboard supports. Use a short piece of linen tape to hold it to one of the side panels. This tape will act as a hinge if you need to fold the container flat.

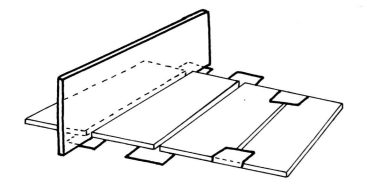

You can use this useful little tray, which is made from display card, for all kinds of things. It is ideal for odds and ends on a desk, but you could also use it for nuts or little biscuits.

1 Begin by making the basic shape for a folded box (see page 14), but so that the sides slope, adjust the corners as shown below. Instead of cutting out corners measuring 90 degrees, the angles are nearer to 30 degrees. Use sharp scissors to cut the corner sections.

2 The display card used makes the tray sturdy enough for everyday use, but it is too stiff to score with the pointed end of a bone folder. You will have to cut halfway through the card with a craft knife before you can bend the sides up. Be careful not to cut all the way through the card.

3 Use adhesive tape to hold the corners together.

Covering the Outside
1 Cover the outside of the tray in a single piece of paper. Use the template of the cardboard to draw the outline and add 12mm (½in) to all four sides.

2 Cut notches in the corners of the paper and apply a coat of paste.

3 Place the tray centrally on the paper and bend the long sides of the paper up and over the rim. Cut away the excess paper in the corners.

4 Bend up the short ends, smoothing the edges down neatly over and into the inside corners. Use your burnisher to smooth out all creases and air bubbles.

Covering the Inside
1 Cover the base, using a piece of paper that is slightly larger than the surface of the base. Press the paper down so that the turned-up edge is even all round and there are no creases or air bubbles.

2 Use individual strips to cover the sides. Cut pieces for the two long sides first, then cover the two short sides, mitring the angles so that the corners fit neatly.

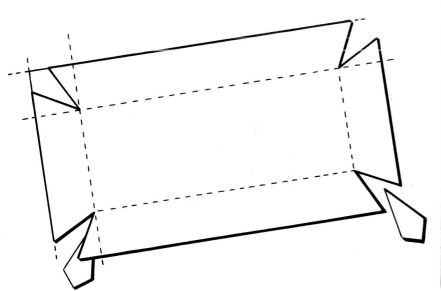

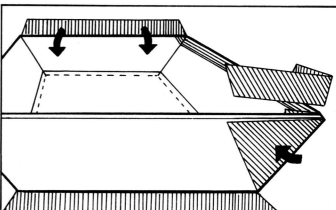

This folder will hold A4 size paper and there is space for a bulldog clip at the top. Because this needs to be fairly strong, use grey bookbinder's board.

1 Follow the dimensions shown below to cut out the separate pieces.

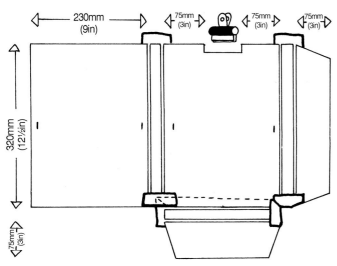

2 Using 38mm (1½in) wide linen tape for the hinges, attach the two large pieces to the spine. The piece with the cut-out section for the bulldog clip should be on the right. Leave a gap of about 15mm (¾in) between the two pieces, using a strip of card to make sure that the gap is equal all the way down.

3 Leave ends of 12mm (½in) of tape at the top and bottom, but do not turn them down until you have removed the spacer card and replaced it with a strip of brown wrapping paper. Turn down the tape.

4 Follow the same procedure to tape the flaps at the right side and bottom of the back panel. Cut the ends of the tape so that it folds down neatly over the brown wrapping paper and over the angles of the flaps.

5 Cover the outside of the front, back and bottom and side flaps with individual pieces of paper. The section around the gap should be covered as shown.

6 Cover the inside with a single sheet of paper. Place the folder under a heavy object and leave to dry.

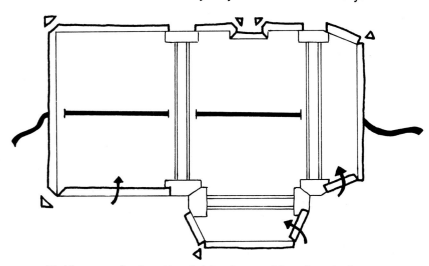

7 You can fasten the folder by making four holes as shown and threading tape through the holes.

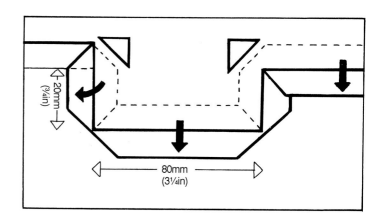

Round box (pages 18-19); pencil box (page 44); Advent calendar (page 46); diagonally opening box with drawers (page 74).

If you want to make a box with separate compartments, the first task is to find the dimensions of the articles you want to put in the compartments so that there is sufficient room for them. For example, you might want to make a box to hold compact discs or the floppy disks you use in your computer or word processor.

We have made a box to hold floppy disks, which measure 90 x 93mm (3½ x 3¾in) and are 3mm (⅛in) thick. So that we can get the disks into and out of the box easily, we have made the end section 100 x 100mm (4 x 4in), and, so that the box will hold a lot of disks, we have made the sides 200mm (8in) long.

The partitions should be lower than the sides of the box, and ours are only 60mm (2½in) high, so that it is easy to see the disks and to remove them. We have made four partitions, which are at intervals of 30mm (1¼in) along the base of the box.

1 Cut out the pieces of card for the base, sides and lid. The front short edge of the base is the same height as the partitions – that is, 60mm (2½in) high. Before gluing the base section to the sides, draw lines on the side pieces to indicate the positions of the partitions.

2 The base and lid of the box are assembled in the same way as the cut box (see page 16).

3 Cover the inside base of the box and the inside of the lid (see page 24).

4 To make the partitions, take a piece of card 60mm (2½in) wide and about 400mm (16in) long and divide it into four equal pieces, each 100mm (4in) long. If you prefer, you can measure the length of these strips

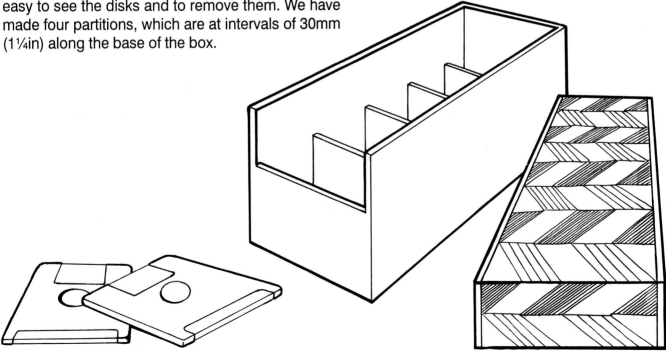

by laying them over the assembled base, as shown below.

5 The partitions should be inserted into the box before it is covered because the covering paper will help to hold the partitions in position. Before you glue the partitions in place, check that they fit exactly. If they are too short they will simply fall over, and if they are too wide they will distort the sides of the box. Apply glue to the bottom and both side edges of each partition, and place them in the box, making sure they align with the pencil lines made in step 1. Leave the glue to dry.

6 Cover the partitions individually. Cut out strips of paper twice the height of the partition and 18mm (¾in) longer. Fold each strip in half lengthways and cut a small triangular section from the centre at both sides. Cut the four bottom corners of each strip to slight angles.

7 Apply paste to one of the strips and place it over the first partition, bending the flaps over the sides in front of and behind the partition and on both sides. Use your burnisher to press down the paper into the corners, and take care that the partition does not move from its upright position.

8 Cover the long sides of the box with single pieces of paper into which you have cut notches to accommodate the partitions. Cover the short ends.

9 Finally, cover the outside of the base and the outside of the lid.

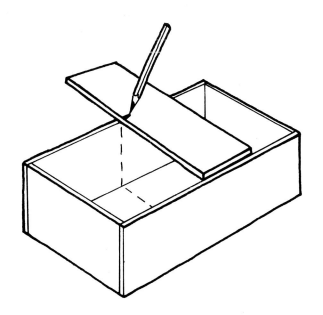

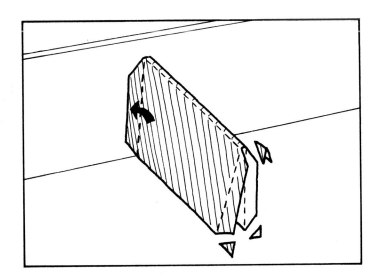

The advantage of making your own pencil box is that you can design it to suit your own belongings. First, decide what you want to keep in it. Then draw the outline of the box on a sheet of scrap paper and lay the items you want to put in the box inside the outline, until you find the most convenient arrangement.

1 Make the base of the box by the cutting method (see page 16) and mark in the position of the partitions.

2 Cut the pieces for the partitions from display card and assemble and cover the inside of the box as described on page 43.

Making the Lid
Several different kinds of lid are suitable for boxes of this kind. If you wish, you can make a standard lid from display card or you can do as we have done and make a folder, with the box glued in position inside.

1 The folder is made from three separate sections. The top and bottom, which are the same size, should be the size of the basic box, but 18mm (about ¾in) longer and 12mm (½in) deeper. The spine should be about 2mm (1/10in) deeper that the box.

2 Cover the three individual pieces before joining them together. Leave to dry under a flat, heavy object.

3 Use narrow linen tape to hold the sections together. Each piece should be about 1.5mm (¹/₁₆in) apart (see page 38) and the tape should be long enough to wrap around the ends by about 12mm (½in).

4 Cover the inside of the folder with a single piece of paper. Leave to dry.

5 Cover the edges with tape, making triangular cuts at the corners so that are mitred neatly.

6 Glue the base of the box inside the folder.

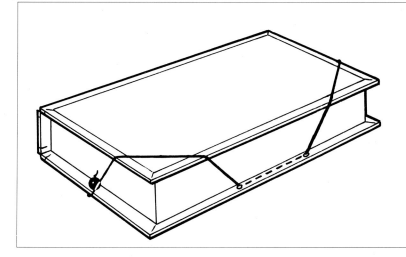

FASTENING THE BOX
Cut four holes with punch pliers as shown, positioning them midway along the short sides and one-third of the way from each corner along the front edge. If you wish, add small metal hole reinforcements. Thread a length of black elastic through the holes, holding it at each end with a small bead.

Tray with sloping sides (page 39); Advent calendar (page 46).

TOYS AND GAMES

Christmas is the time of year when many families take time to cut and paste. If you begin early enough, you can make an Advent calendar out of small box drawers. Although it is a time-consuming and complicated project to make, you will be able to use it year after year.

Glue the finished calendar into a folder, in the same way as you made the folder for the pencil box on page 44. Make the folder first.

ADVENT CALENDAR [41][45]

Making the Folder
Use 2mm ($^1/_{10}$in) thick card or grey bookbinder's board and 18mm ($^3/_4$in) linen tape for the hinges.

1 Cut out the five sections of the folder, using the measurements shown below.

2 So that the folder will close, each section should be 2mm ($^1/_{10}$in) apart; use a piece of card as described on page 40 to make sure the sides are parallel.

3 Use lengths of tape that fold over the top and bottom by 12mm ($^1/_2$in).

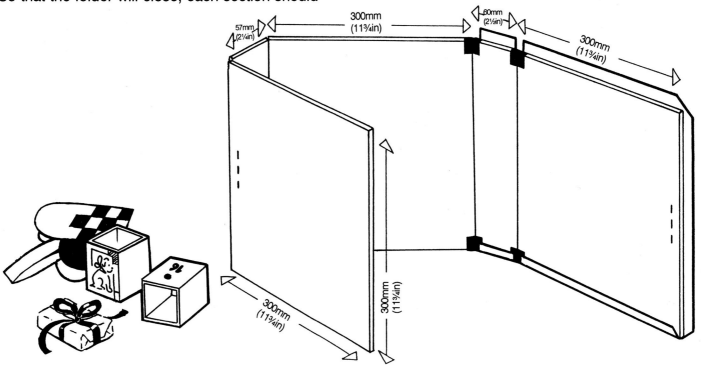

57mm (2¼in)

300mm (11¾in)

60mm (2½in)

300mm (11¾in)

300mm (11¾in)

300mm (11¾in)

ATTACHING THE RIBBONS

You should attach the ribbons that fasten the folder before you cover the inside. Use a small chisel or your craft knife to cut three slots in the front sections as shown in the illustration.

You will need six narrow ribbons, each about 50cm (20in) long. Thread each ribbon through a slot from the front and hold it in place with a spot of adhesive. You can make the ribbons extra secure by gluing a small piece of brown wrapping paper over the ends of the ribbon.

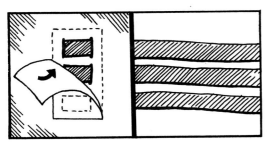

4 Cover the outside of each section individually. Each piece of paper should be large enough to allow 12mm (½in) turn in on all free sides.

5 Place the folder under a flat, heavy object and allow to dry.

Covering the Inside

1 Cover the two narrow sections with plain paper, which should be 20mm (¾in) wider than each section. Paste the paper down so that each piece covers the joints. Use your burnisher to press the paper down firmly, especially into the grooves, so that it does not come away when the folder is opened and closed.

2 Cut two pieces of Christmas wrapping paper, each 280 x 280mm (11 x 11in) for the two front sections. Paste them down, making sure they are positioned centrally on the card (see illustration on page 45).

3 Leave the folder to dry under a heavy object.

Making the Box

The large box has partitions that create the small compartments for the drawers. Make the box, with a base and four sides, from 2mm (^{1}/₁₀in) thick cardboard using the cutting method (page 16) and to the dimensions shown below.

1 Glue the base and sides together to form the basic box shape.

2 While the box is drying, cut the partitions. You need four long strips, which are glued on horizontally, and 20 short strips, to make the vertical divisions.

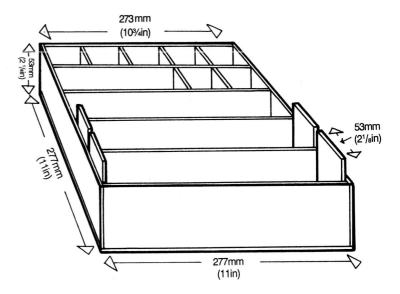

3 So that all the compartments are exactly the same size, it is a good idea to cut some spare sections of card before you begin. Measure these so that they are exactly 53mm (2¹/₈in) and use them to check the position of the partitions.

4 Glue the long, horizontal strips in place first, following the method described on pages 42–3, then glue in the short vertical dividers.

Covering the Box

1 Cover the front edges of all the short vertical dividers with strips 18mm (¾in) wide as described on page 22. Remember to fold each strip in half lengthways before pasting it down.

2 Use long strips, also 18mm (¾in) wide, to cover the horizontal dividers, cutting notches in them so that they fit neatly over the vertical pieces of card.

3 Cover the outside edges of the box. Use strips 60mm (2½) wide, allowing 12mm (½in) to turn under the box on each piece and an extra 12mm (½in) at each end of the two long ends. Cut the short ends to the exact length (see page 25).

4 Glue the covered box to the centre section of the folder. Close the folder around the box so that you can leave it to dry under a heavy object.

Making the Drawers

There is room for 25 drawers in your Advent calendar, so you might decide to seal the middle compartment. Alternatively, you could decide to put an extra gift in it for Christmas Eve. Make the drawers from box card according to the folding method (see page 14). Each box should measure 50 x 50mm (2 x 2in).

1 Cut all the pieces you will need for the drawers and cover them on the inside before assembling them.

2 Cover the outside of the base and three sides with plain paper.

3 Cover the back of each box with Christmas wrapping paper. You can either use lots of different, small motifs, or one large pattern, arranged in jigsaw fashion. The patterned side is revealed as each day a different box is turned around.

4 Make a hole with punch pliers in the front of each drawer and push through a small wing paper fastener, with the knob on the outside so that it resembles a knob. Draw or paint numbers from 1 to 24 on the drawers.

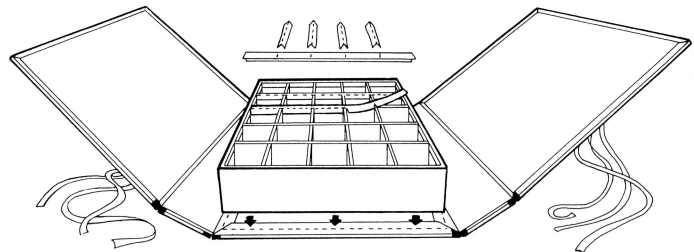

Chinese boxes (page 50).

It was the Chinese who first devised the series of decorated boxes that fit inside each other. We have made four boxes, but you can, of course, make as many as you wish – it will just depend how patient you are.

The boxes are made from display card and these are the dimensions of the four boxes.

TIP

As you cut the parts out, it is a good idea to label them. You will find it easier than trying to remember which bit belongs to which box.

Base

1 piece 192 x 192mm (7½ x 7½in)
2 pieces 192 x 88mm (7½ x 3½in)
2 pieces 189 x 88mm (7¼ x 3½in)

1 piece 162 x 162mm (6¼ x 6¼in)
2 pieces 162 x 78mm (6¼ x 3in)
2 pieces 159 x 78mm (6⅛ x 3in)

1 piece 132 x 132mm (5¼ x 5¼in)
2 pieces 132 x 68mm (5¼ x 2¾in)
2 pieces 129 x 68mm (5⅛ x 2¾in)

1 piece 102 x 102mm (4 x 4in)
2 pieces 102 x 58mm (4 x 2¼in)
2 pieces 99 x 58mm (3¾ x 2¼in)

Lid

1 piece 200 x 200mm (7¾ x 7¾in)
2 pieces 200 x 90mm (7¾ x 3¾in)
2 pieces 197 x 90mm (7⅝ x 3¾in)

1 piece 170 x 170mm (6¾ x 6¾in)
2 pieces 170 x 80mm (6¾ x 3¼in)
2 pieces 167 x 80mm (6½ x 3¼in)

1 piece 140 x 140mm (5½ x 5½in)
2 pieces 140 x 70mm (5½ x 2¾in)
2 pieces 137 x 70mm (5¼ x 2¾in)

1 piece 110 x 110mm (4¼ x 4¼in)
2 pieces 110 x 60mm (4¼ x 2⅝in)
2 pieces 107 x 60mm (4⅛ x 2⅝in)

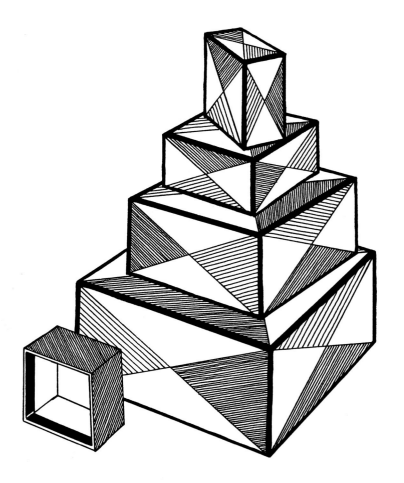

Assemble the boxes as described on page 16.

The covering used for the box is based on the use of four colours – red, yellow, blue and green, combined with each other. The illustration on page 49 shows how the colours are used, and the base sections and lids of each box having matching colour combinations.

Cover the inside of the boxes as described on pages 24–5. The outsides are covered with triangles of the four chosen colours.

1 Draw the different sections on to tracing paper. Divide each piece into four by drawing in the diagonal lines.

2 Transfer the triangles to the coloured paper and cut out the appropriate triangles.

3 Paste the triangles on the outside of the boxes, making sure that they are positioned accurately so that the triangles meet in the centre.

4 Cover the edges of each box with strips of black paper (see page 22).

5 Finally, paste strips of each colour to the inside of the lids; the strips should be 12mm (½in) wide and should be positioned about 2mm (¹/₁₀in) from the top edge.

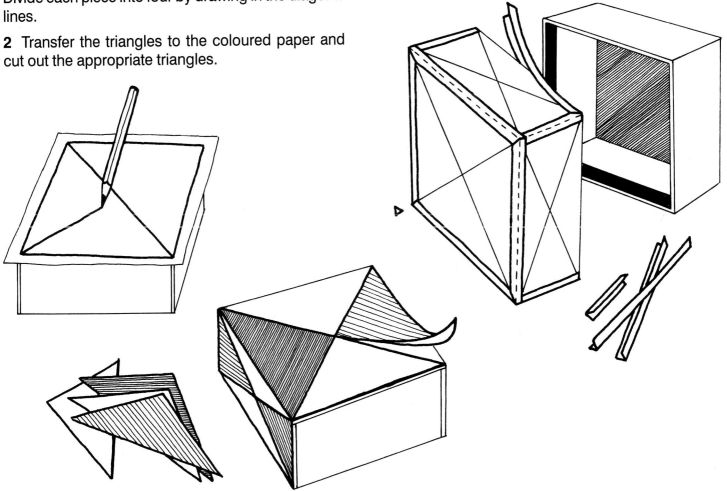

The chest is made from several small drawer boxes, which are glued on top of each other. A single drawer box consists of an outer case with a drawer that slides in and out, rather like the tray of a matchbox. You must make sure that the case is large enough for the drawer to move freely and smoothly in and out without actually falling out.

Making a Drawer Box

The drawer should be made out of box card as described on page 14. The base should be 140 x 140mm (5½ x 5½in), while the sides should be 30mm (1¼in) high. The bottom of the drawers are often used as game boards, and these should be covered before the drawer is assembled. Some ideas for games – a chess board, maze puzzles, solitaire and a ball game – are given on the pages that follow.

Make the case from a single piece of box card, 350 x 145mm (13¾ x 5¾in). The base and top should measure 145 x 143mm (5¾ x 5⅝in), and the sides

should be 32mm (1³/₈in) deep. Draw the measurements on the card so that you can fold the edges in the exact positions. We made five drawers and cases. Cover the insides and outsides of the drawers as described for the individual games.

Hold the five cases together with strips of adhesive tape and cut two pieces of card, 145 x 164mm (5¾ x 6½in), to glue to the sides.

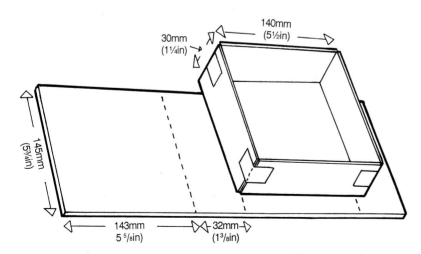

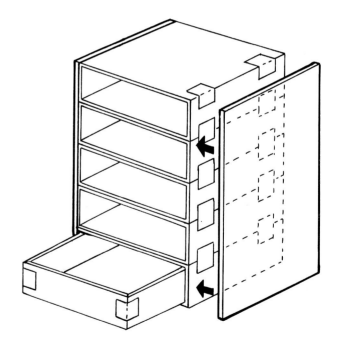

Games chest (pages 52-9).

Cover all the open edges of the cases, front and back, with strips of paper 18mm (¾in) wide. Then use a single gaily patterned paper to cover the top, base and sides of the chest. If the paper does not have a "right way up", use a single piece around the sides, top and base to give extra stability. Otherwise, use four single pieces as described on page 25. You can now insert the drawers.

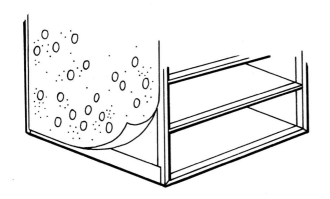

four single pieces as described on page 25.

DRAWER HANDLES

You could use tiny dice, glued on to the centre of the front and back of each of the drawers so that they can be pulled out from either the front or the back of the case. An alternative is to use metal paper fasteners, which have wings that open on the inside. On page 73 we explain how to use metal drawer knobs.

On page 73 we explain how to use metal drawer knobs.

CHESS BOARD AND PIECES [53]

Chess is one of the most popular games in the world, even though it is so complex. We used the base of one of the drawers in the chest for the board, and you should decorate it before you turn up and cover the sides.

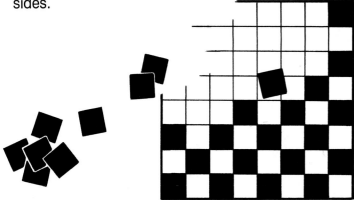

1 Paint the inside of the drawer with acrylic paint. Leave it to dry.

2 Make the squares to cover the base of the drawer. You will need 64 squares, eight in each direction, and you should cut them from plastic. Glue them on individually.

3 Join the corners of the box with adhesive tape, then cover the outside with paper.

Make the chess pieces out of 12mm (½in) wooden dowel. Some of the pieces are slanted tops and you should follow the outlines on page 55. When you saw the wood, hold it firmly in a vice or use a mitre box. Paint the pieces with acrylic paint.

you should follow the outlines on page 55.

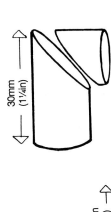

Knights are made from two sawn sections glued together.

The bishop is sawn at an angle and has a vertical notch cut out from the centre.

30mm (1¼in)

10mm (⅜in)

Pawns are sawn at an angle and painted in two colours.

20mm (¾in)

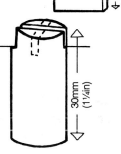

30mm (1¼in)

15mm (⅝in)

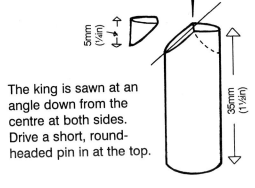

5mm (¼in)

The king is sawn at an angle down from the centre at both sides. Drive a short, round-headed pin in at the top.

35mm (1½in)

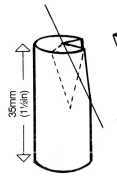

20mm (¾in)

35mm (1½in)

5mm (¼in)

The queen is made by sawing off four triangular sections.

Rooks are sawn straight off across the top and then a cross-shaped notch is cut into the top.

30mm (1¼in)

It's great fun making maze puzzles and just as much fun playing with them. You can roll one or more balls around the maze – the more balls there are, the harder it is to reach the target. The illustrations will give you some ideas of how the base of the drawers in your games chess can be decorated, but you can create your own designs, especially if you use the grid shown below.

4 Instead of covering the maze with paper, you could paint with interior with acrylic paint in appropriate colours.

5 Colour the top edge of the dividing card with a felt-tipped pen in a contrasting colour. Cut an arrow and a star out of coloured paper and glue them in position to represent the start and finish.

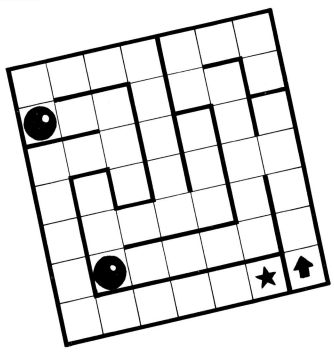

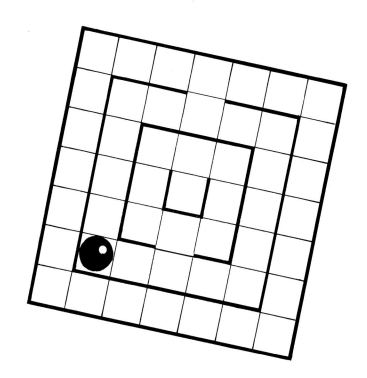

1 Draw the maze in the centre of the base of the drawer. Where the lines meet the sides of the box, extend the lines to the edge of the card.

2 Make the partitions from a piece of card 20mm (¾in) wide. Cut them to the appropriate lengths and glue them in position (see page 43).

3 Use adhesive tape to join the corners of the drawer.

Games chest (pages 52-9).

The object of solitaire is to finish with a pin in the centre hole of the board, and the game is one that can be played by just one person. You can only move a pin over another pin by moving in a straight line, either backwards or forwards. You remove the pin you have jumped over and you should end up with just one pin left on the board.

1 Cut a piece of cork or close-textured foam rubber that is at least 6mm (¼in) deep that is the same dimensions as the inside base of the drawer – i.e., 140 x 140mm (5½ x 5½in).

2 Cut out a piece of coloured card, also 140 x 140mm (5½ x 5½in). On the back of the square draw an 8 x 8 grid, with lines 17mm (¾in) apart in both directions. Make holes at the points shown in the illustration.

3 Turn over the card and stick white ring reinforcements around the holes (see the illustration on page 57).

4 Cover the inside of the base of the drawer and use adhesive tape to stick the corners together.

5 Glue the foam rubber or cork in the base of the drawer and stick the card on top.

6 Cover the outside of the box.

7 Insert 32 pins of the kind used on notice boards into the holes, leaving the centre one empty.

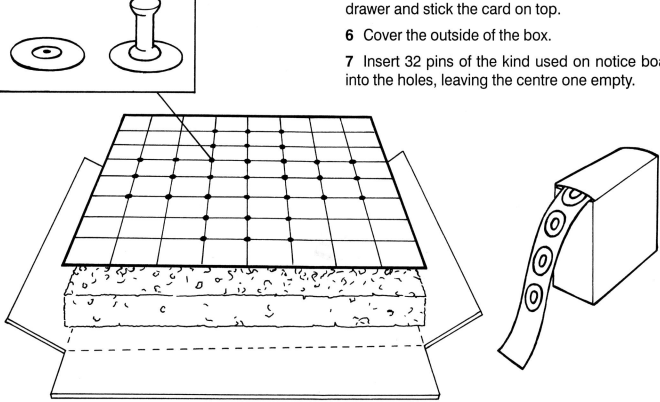

This is one of the easiest games to make and is great fun to play. The board is nothing more than a picture with holes punched in it. The object of the game is to get the balls into the holes and to keep them all in place at the same time.

1 Choose a suitable picture from a magazine or poster or draw a picture yourself. The picture should be slightly larger than the base of the box so that it will turn up all around the edges.

2 Paste the picture in the bottom of the drawer before you assemble it. Place it under a heavy object until the paste is dry.

3 Use a tube punch to make the holes in the picture. The smaller the holes, the harder it is to balance the balls in position.

4 Cover the edges of the box around the picture with plain paper, then hold the corners together with adhesive tape.

5 Cover the outside of the drawer with coloured paper.

MAGIC BOXES

Magic is an endless source of fascination for adults and children alike, and in this section we show how you can make your own magic boxes. Magic boxes usually contain all kinds of mysterious things – they can have secret compartments that no one knows about or they can be used for tricks that no one would have thought possible.

LOOK! I'VE FOUND A FINGER [61]

This trick is certainly not for people of a nervous disposition. The magician tells the audience that he or she is going to show them a very gruesome trick and holds up a little box with a sliding compartment. The magician slowly pulls the box open – and the audience cannot believe its eyes, for in the box they see a severed, bloody finger, resting on cotton wool.

The secret behind this macabre trick is, of course, nothing like as gruesome. Here is how it is done. You make a box with a sliding compartment as described on page 52 to the dimensions shown below. If you wanted to cheat a little, you could use an empty, household size matchbox.

1 Cut a hole in the base of the drawer through which you can stick your finger.

2 Cut an oblong out of the outer case as shown in the illustration.

3 Before you begin the trick, fill the box with cotton wool and paint the bottom of your finger red.

4 Stick your finger through the hole in the base and slide the case over. You're now ready to perform the trick!

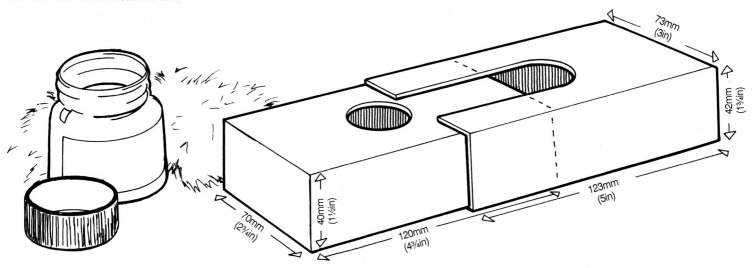

73mm (3in)

42mm (1¾in)

40mm (1½in)

70mm (2¾in)

120mm (4¾in)

123mm (5in)

Magic boxes (pages 60-4).

The magician shows the audience two dice and a small box with a sliding compartment. He or she shows that the box is empty, places the dice inside it and shakes the box so that the audience can hear the dice rattling around inside. Then the magician tells the audience that when the box is opened, the numbers showing on the dice will be 2 and 6. The box is opened and, lo and behold, the dice show 2 and 6.

For this trick you will need a box of the kind described on page 60. Cover the outside with a brightly coloured paper but leave the inside plain.

SECRET!

Part of the secret behind this trick is that the drawer section is divided into two equal compartments with a central partition. In addition, you will need four dice. Two of these are glued into one of the compartments so that the numbers 2 and 6 are uppermost. Slide the drawer into the case, and you are ready to start the trick.

Push the drawer open by about a third so that the audience can see the empty compartment (remember to hold the box the right way round). Place the two loose dice in the compartment and close it. Shake the box and tell the audience the numbers on the dice. Before you open the box, turn it round without being seen and slide open the drawer to reveal the two dice.

This really will fox your audience, but remember to hide it away afterwards.

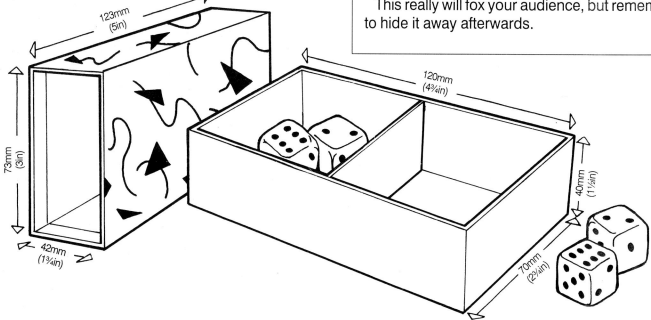

123mm (5in)

73mm (3in)

42mm (1¾in)

120mm (4¾in)

40mm (1½in)

70mm (2¾in)

The magician stands holding a red box. He or she takes the lid off the box to reveal a blue box inside – so the blue box must, clearly, be smaller than the red box. The magician takes out the blue box and puts the lid on the red box, then, looking mysterious, places the red box inside the blue one and puts the lid on. How did that happen?

To make the boxes you need to use display card, cut to the dimensions shown here. Make the boxes as described on page 16 and cover them as explained on page 24.

Two base sections
2 bases 120 x 130mm (4¾ x 5¼in)
4 sides 130 x 110mm (4¾ x 4¼in)
4 sides 117 x 110mm (4 ⅝ x 4¼in)

Two lid sections
2 bases 126 x 136mm (5 ⅛ x 5½in)
4 sides 136 x 110mm (5½ x 4¼in)
4 sides 123 x 110mm (5 x 4¼in)

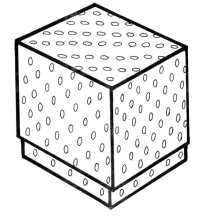

1

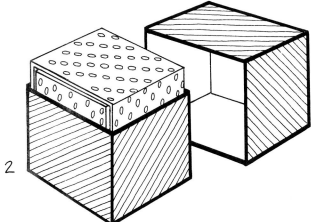

2

SECRET!

Part of the secret behind this trick lies in the fact that the boxes are the same size. They consist of a base and a lid of equal height, but when the outer box is closed, the lid does not go all the way down to the base, as can be seen in figure 1.

When the lid is removed, as you can see from figure 2, the box inside is lying on its side and the base and lid fit snugly right over each other. The audience doesn't notice this unless they are aware of what is going to happen.

Take out the inner box and place the lid over the outer one. This time it should go all the way down to the base. Place the box that was previously on the outside into the box that had been on the inside, placing the box on its side as shown in figure 2. Put the lid on the outer box as shown in figure 1.

The magician shows the audience a large book and explains that it is a very ancient book that contains lots of secret tricks. The magician opens the book and something totally unexpected happens – a large die jumps out from the pages, even though the book itself is quite solid! The die is made from cardboard, but you can press it flat and the moment you take the pressure off, it folds out and becomes a "solid" die.

1 Make the die from six pieces of grey bookbinder's board, each measuring 70 x 70mm (2¾x 2¾in). Paint the pieces black or cover them with black self-adhesive paper or cardboard.

2 Use small, adhesive marker dots for the white spots on the die (you can buy these from stationery shops).

3 In addition to the six pieces of board you will need two identical sections of strong black card, cut as shown in the illustration below.

4 When you have cut out the pieces of card, score in the fold lines with the point of your bone folder.

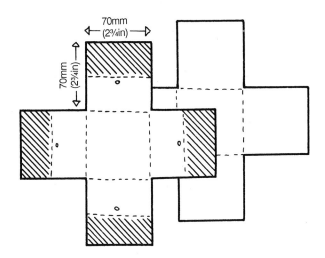

5 Use a plier-type hole punch to make four holes in one of the pieces of card as shown in the illustration. You could strengthen the holes by sticking a small piece of linen tape over the area before you punch the hole through.

6 Glue the card with the holes to the back of the side of the die with one spot on it.

7 Glue the other piece of card to the back of the side of the die with six spots on it. (Remember that the spots on the opposite sides of a die always total seven.)

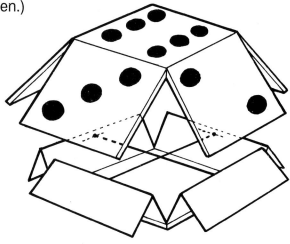

8 Glue the two pieces of card together, with the pieces of board on the outside. Smear adhesive on the outer surfaces of the card as indicated in the illustration.

9 When the adhesive is dry, run some pieces of elastic through the holes in the card as shown in the illustration. The lengths of elastic should cross each other and can be held around small pins.

When the die is not in use, do not leave it squashed flat because this will strain the holes and wear out the elastic.

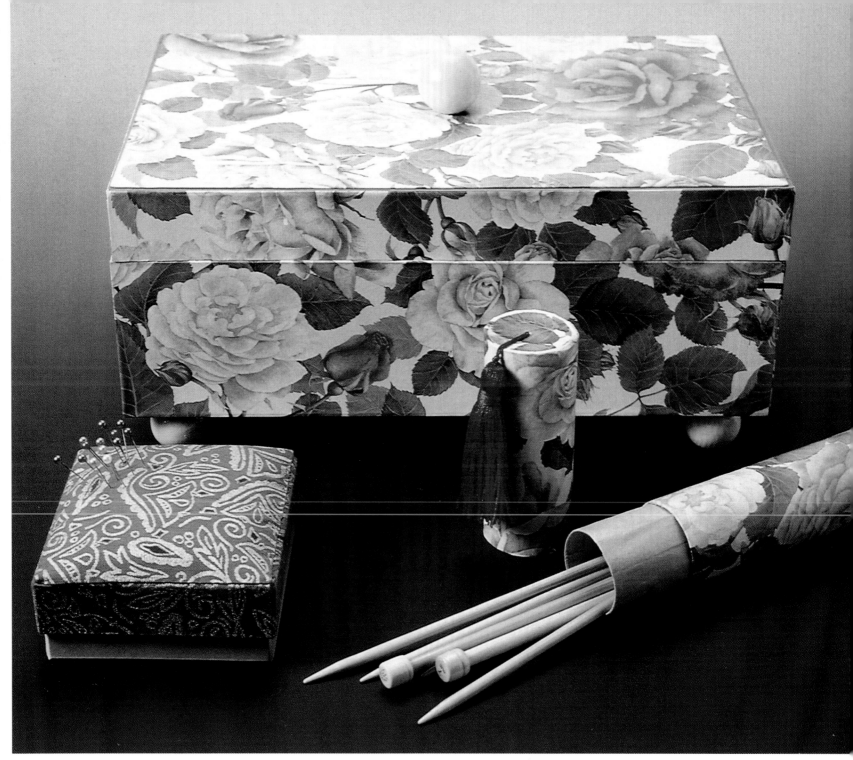

Needlework accessories (pages 66-72).

NEEDLEWORK ACCESSORIES

SEWING BOX [65][69]

If you enjoy needlework and do a great deal, you will find a needlework box like this essential. There is room for everything you use – scissors, your tape measure, knitting needles, cotton and so on. There are also special boxes for buttons, pins and needles. Even if you do not want to make the whole box in one go, you can start with a small box. If you make one box at a time, it won't take you long to complete the whole work box.

Because the sewing box consists of several small boxes, it is important that the boxes are placed in exactly the right position within the box, and all the measurements have been tailored to allow the various boxes to fit neatly into the overall box. However, you must always remember to take the thickness of the cardboard into account, and it is a good idea to make a plan on a piece of paper before you begin to cut out the pieces from cardboard to check that the dimensions are accurate.

The sewing box itself is made using the cutting method (see page 16), and you should use 2mm ($1/10$in) thick cardboard – calendar board or grey bookbinder's board. The lid is hinged in place, and this is described on page 67.

Both the base section and the lid consist of five sections, and the measurements are shown in the illustration below.

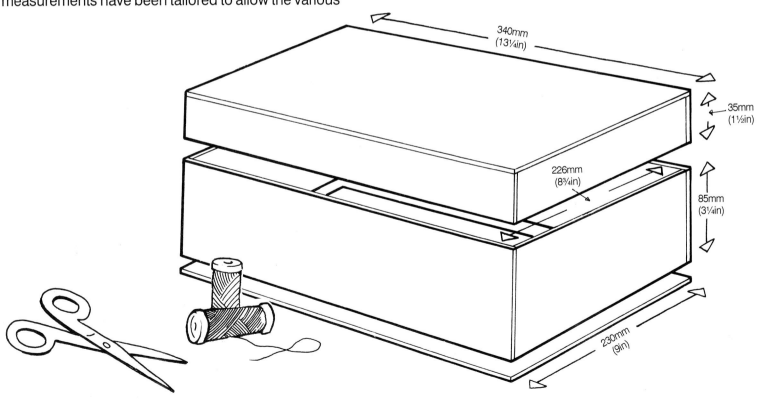

1 Assemble the base and lid and cover the external sides as described on page 25. You should cover the base, top and the back of the base and the lid only when you have added the hinge.

2 Make a hinge from a piece of mull (see page 11) measuring 50 x 340mm (2 x 13¼in). Place the lid on top of the base as shown in the illustration and glue on the mull where the two sections meet.

3 Cut a piece of brown wrapping paper the same size as the mull and paste it over the fabric. The paper helps not only to hold the mull in place but also to disguise the shape of the material, which would otherwise be visible through the covering. Leave to dry before raising the lid.

4 When the paste is dry, open the box completely, supporting the lid so that it does not strain the hinge. Paste a piece of brown wrapping paper over the inside edge of the lid and base. Use clothes pegs or bulldog clips to hold the paper in place while the paste dries.

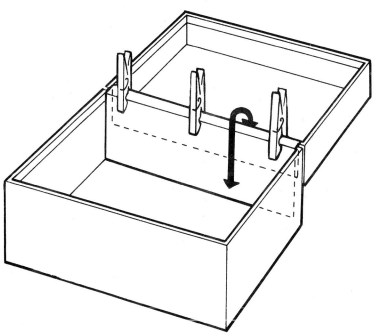

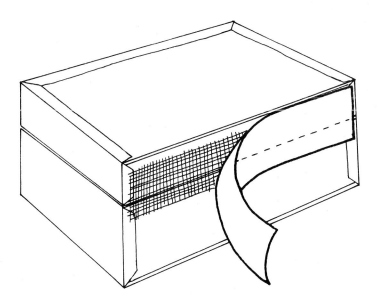

5 Cover the inside of the box as described on page 24, and also cover the base, top and back of the box. You can cover the inside of the box with the same paper as you use for the outside or you might prefer to use a contrasting shade. If you don't use the same paper, it is a good idea to allow the paper used on the outside to be visible for about 5mm (¼in) right round the inside edge of the box.

RETAINING RIBBON

To stop the hinge wearing out and falling to pieces, you should attach a length of silk ribbon to stop the lid from falling backwards.

Make a hole in the centre of the upper left side of the base, about 12mm (½in) down, and make another hole in the centre of the lower left side of the lid. Cut a length of ribbon that will hold the lid open at a slight angle, and fasten the ribbon in place with two metal studs.

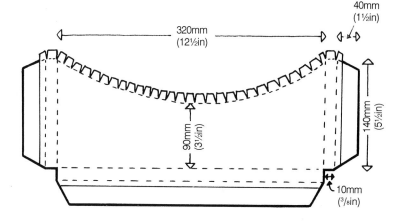

Pocket

Make a pocket for the inside of the lid so that you can store knitting patterns and sewing instructions.

1 Cut the pocket from box card to the measurements shown in the diagram. Cover the card with paper, and cut a series of notches along the curved edge as described in the section on covering round boxes (see page 27).

2 Place the pocket under a heavy, flat object until the paste is dry, then score in the fold lines.

3 Bend the glue flaps round and apply adhesive to the flaps. Glue the pocket to the inside of the lid.

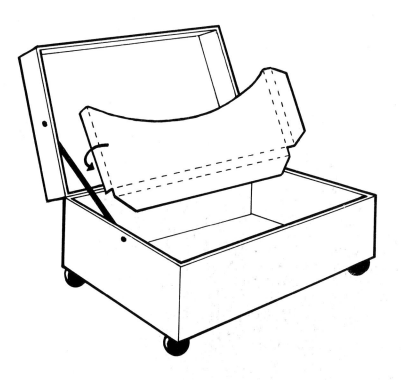

FEET AND HANDLE

Finally, remember to give the sewing box some feet and a handle. You should use four small and one large wooden balls. The balls for the feet should be about 15mm (½in) across and should be glued to each corner. The large ball can be up to 35mm (1¼in) in diameter, and it should be glued in the centre of the lid.

Needlework accessories (pages 66-72).

If you want to divide up the sewing box you can, if you wish, make fixed compartments as we did with the diskette holder (see page 43). However, you will have greater flexibility if, instead of fixed compartments, you use several small boxes that you can move around as you wish.

Rectangular boxes without a lid are ideal for the bottom of a work box, and you can place them side by side or one on top of the other. The container for sewing cottons has partitions that make it suitable for storing reels of cotton, and you can adjust the position of the partitions to suit the size of the reels.

So that the boxes are sturdy and long-lasting, make them from thick cardboard and use the cutting method (see page 16). If you use cardboard that is 2mm ($^1/_{10}$in) thick – bookbinder's board or calendar board, for example – you can follow the dimensions shown in the diagram.

1 Cover the box with plain paper, but do not try to cover the whole box with a single, large piece of paper. A box as large as this can be difficult to manage. Cut paper for the long sides first, allowing 12mm (½in) extra for the edges all round.

2 When you have cut the paper for the sides, cover the ends, and here you need allow an extra 12mm (½in) for the top and bottom only.

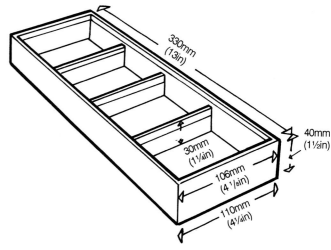

BOX WITH CURVED SIDES

A four-sided box need not always have straight edges. Curved edges often look very elegant, but you must make a template so that both sides are identical.

The height of the sides shown here vary by 20mm (about ¾in) – that is, the end pieces are 60mm (2½in) high while the long sides curve upwards from 60mm (2½in) at the ends to 80mm (3¼in) in the centre.

1 Cover the box with plain paper.

2 When you cover the curved edge, cut a series of small notches as explained on page 27.

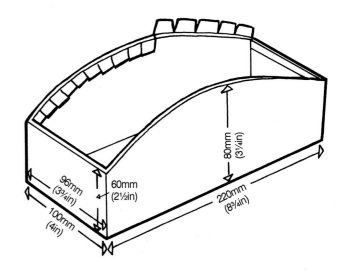

BUTTON BOX [69]

The button box is made from calendar board or grey bookbinder's board using the cutting method (see page 16). If you wish, you can make the box with separate compartments. Because the lid is going to be sprayed with bronze paint, it should be covered with brown wrapping paper to make a durable, cover.

1 When you have made the base and lid, assemble on the lid a collage of articles representing the contents – buttons, press-studs, hooks and eyes etc.

2 Glue the individual items in place with spots of adhesive and leave to dry.

3 Following the manufacturer's instructions and working outdoors, spray the top of the lid. You will probably get better results if you apply several coats.

4 Cover the base with plain paper.

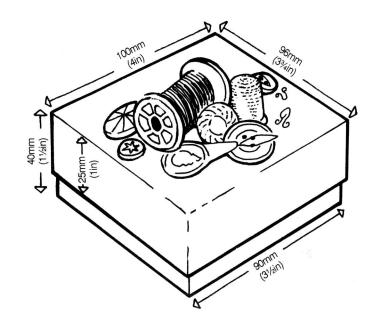

KNITTING NEEDLE HOLDER [65]

The knitting needle holder is made from two cardboard tubes. The long tube comes from a roll of kitchen towel and the shorter one from a roll of toilet paper.

1 Make the top and bottom by cutting two circles, the same diameter as the tubes, from box card.

2 Glue the circles in place, one at the end of each tube, then cover the tubes as described on page 27.

3 Glue a round liner into the longer tube.

Attach a tassle by a piece of fine cord through a hole in the centre of the lid and hold it in place by a button on the inside of the lid.

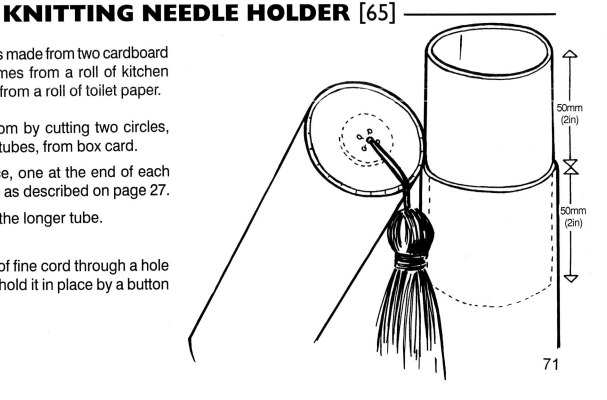

PINCUSHION BOX [65][69]

This box is made to exactly the same measurements as the button box (see page 71). You can use the padded lid to hold pins and needles and you can keep your thimbles and packets of needles inside the box.

When you have made the lid and base, cover the base, inside and out, with paper. The lid is going to be covered with material, and you should choose a fine-weave cotton or linen.

1 Cut a strip of material that is about 20mm (¾in) longer than the distance around all four sides. It should be 20mm (¾in) wider than the depth of the lid.

2 Apply a thin coat of clear, all-purpose adhesive to the sides of the lid, and stick the fabric around the lid so that it is centrally positioned.

3 The material should start and end at a corner. Turn under the loose end and either glue it or stitch it down with a row of tiny over-stitches.

4 On the bottom edge of the lid cut triangles of fabric from the corners and turn the edges up into the lid, where they can be glued down. Do not glue the fabric down to the top surface of the lid, but simply fold it over neatly, mitring the corners.

5 Cut one or two pieces of wadding to fit the top of the box and cut out another piece of material that is 12mm (½in) larger all round than the top of the box.

6 Turn in the hem of the first short side, creasing it down with your thumbnail or ironing it if necessary, and stitch it to the short side of the lid (at A).

7 Place the wadding on top of the box, turn in the hems of the two long sides (at B and C) and use tiny over-stitches to hold the two sides in place, making sure that the fabric is smooth over the wadding. Finally, sew the last open seam, D.

8 If you wish, trim the box by gluing or sewing a length of braid around the upper edge of the lid.

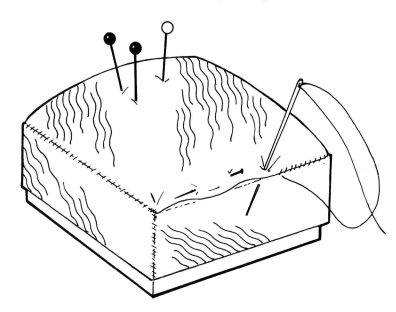

OTHER BOXES
DRAWERS WITH ROUND BOXES [77]

Although it looks impressive, this useful project is simply made by gluing round boxes on top of a flat chest of three opening drawers. The boxes can be used to hold pencils, pens or brushes, and the drawers are perfect for paper clips, notelets and so on.

Making the Drawers
Make the little chest of drawers as you would a flat drawer box (see page 52) but make partitions for three drawers. The drawers do not need to be the same size –you could vary their width according to what you want to keep in them. If you want the drawers to last, you must use a robust cardboard such as calendar board or grey bookbinder's board.

We used small drawer knobs, which finish off the drawers perfectly. These are sold in some craft shops, especially those that supply materials for making dolls' houses and dolls' house furniture.

Making the Boxes
You can make the round boxes from cardboard tubes. We made two different sizes, and if you want to make something similar to the boxes illustrated on page 77, you will need two small tubes and one larger one. We fitted the larger tube with a lid with a knob.

1 Cut the tubes to length with a small saw or with a craft knife. If the edges are frayed and ragged, smooth them with fine sandpaper.

2 Cover the boxes as described on page 27.

3 Make the lid for the large box from two circles of thick cardboard. One of the circles should be as large as the external diameter of the tube and the other one should be smaller so that it can be inserted inside the tube.

4 Cover both cardboard discs with circles of paper. Each paper circle should be about 12mm (½in) larger than the disc it is covering. Cut a series of notches around the paper and paste them in position, bending each piece down carefully and smoothly. Glue the two circles together so that the turned-down edges are in the middle of the sandwich.

5 Use a nail or awl to make a hole through the centre of the lid and attach a knob.

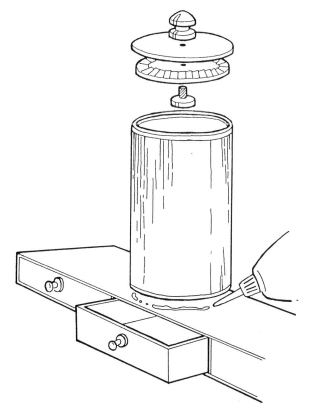

This little box with drawers can be used to hold lots of small things that you have on your desk. You could also use the box to hold jewellery or make-up, and the design was, in fact, inspired by a cosmetics case used by Japanese geishas.

The box consists of two triangular sections, which are held together at the back by a hinge made of linen tape or mull. If you use mull, remember to paste some brown wrapping paper over the fabric (see page 67). Inside the box are five small drawers, the bottom one of which is fixed in place.

1 The two triangular boxes are assembled from eight pieces cut out of display card; follow the dimensions shown in the diagram. Use two triangles for the top section and two for the bottom section.

2 Make the boxes by the cutting method (see page 16).

3 When the glue is dry, hold them tightly together and glue on the hinge of linen tape or mull (covered by brown wrapping paper) all the way down the back. Do not open the box until the hinge is completely dry.

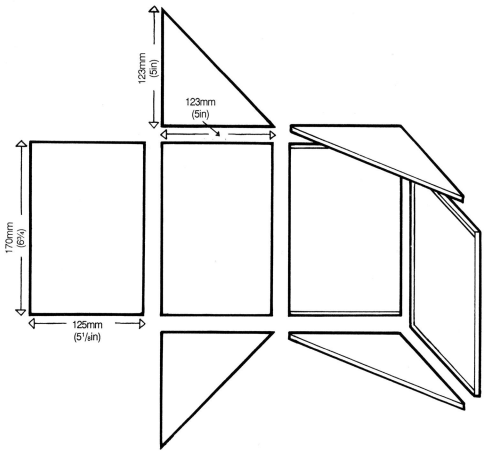

Covering the Outside

Cover the outside of the box first. Use a sheet of paper that will go all the way round, and if you have followed the sizes shown on page 74, you will need a piece about 195 x 525mm (7¾ x 20½in), including 12mm (½in) for folding down on all sides (see the diagram below).

1 Cut small triangles from the centre of the back and from all the corners so that the paper fits neatly.

2 Make sure that the paper lies smoothly all over the surface, especially over the front closing sections.

3 Cut four triangles from thin card the same size as the top and base and cover one side of these with paper. Glue them over the triangles to cover the turned-down edges of the paper used for the sides.

Covering the Inside

Before you cover the inside, glue a strip of brown wrapping paper, about 30mm (1¼in) wide, over the join in the back.

1 Cut triangular sections for the top and bottom. These should be slightly larger than the actual top and base so that there is a small turned-up edge all round. Cut out a small triangle from the apex of each triangle so that they lie neatly against the edge.

2 Cover the sides of each half with separate pieces of paper, cut to fit exactly.

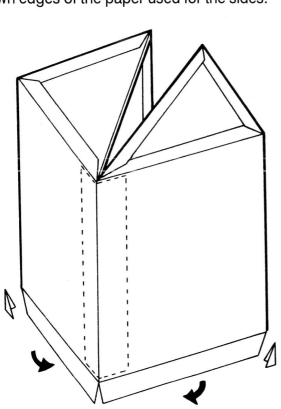

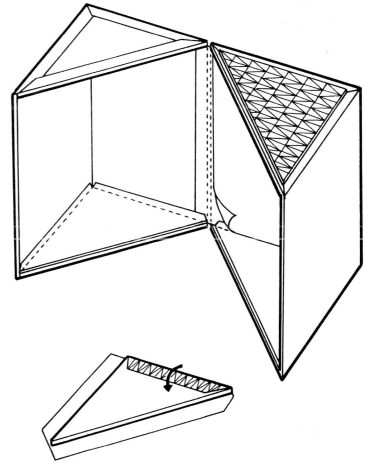

Making the Drawers

Each of the drawers measures 120 x 120 (4¾ x 4¾in) and is 30mm (1¼in) deep. They are made by the cutting method and glued together, and each has small partitions in various positions as shown in the illustrations.

The bottom drawer is glued in place into the base of one of the triangles, and the other drawers rest on

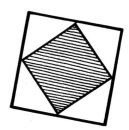
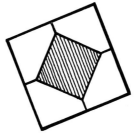

top of each other, so that you can pull them out as you need the things kept in them.

Cover the drawers inside and out. We used a paper that matches the colours used for the outside of the box, which gives a pleasing appearance. Then glue the bottom box to the base of one of the triangular sections. Make sure you allow enough room for the box to close by placing two pieces of card under the drawer before you glue it down.

FASTENING THE BOX

The best way to keep the box closed is to use an old-fashioned envelope seal. It is made from two thick cardboard discs, cut out with a 15mm (about ½in) tube punch. In the centre of each disc you should make a hole with a plier-style hole punch, then make holes in corresponding places in the front of both closing sections of the box, about 20mm (¾in) from the edge (see the illustration on page 77). Fasten the discs with metal rivets and tie a length of strong thread around one of the rivets. To fasten the box, wind the thread around the other rivet as shown in the diagram.

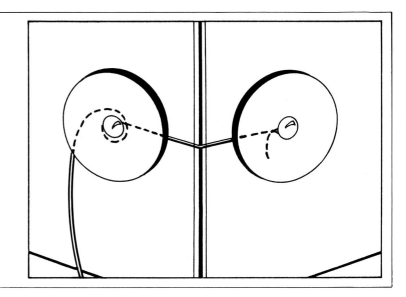

Drawers with round boxes (page 73); diagonally opening box with drawers (page 74).